D1368130

PUBLIC RELATIONS FOR THE ENTREPRENEUR AND THE GROWING BUSINESS

How to Use
Public Relations
to Increase Visibility
and Create Opportunities
for You and Your Company

by
NORMAN R. SODERBERG

PROBUS PUBLISHING COMPANY
Chicago, Illinois

This publication is designed to provide accurate and authoritative information in regard to the subject matter covered. It is sold with the understanding that the publisher is not engaged in rendering legal, accounting or other professional service. If legal advice or other expert assistance is required, the services of a competent professional person should be sought.

FROM A DECLARATION OF PRINCIPLES JOINTLY ADOPTED BY A COMMITTEE OF THE AMERICAN BAR ASSOCIATION AND A COMMITTEE OF PUBLISHERS.

Library of Congress Cataloging in Publication Data

Soderberg, Norman R.

Public relations for the entrepreneur and the growing business.

Bibliography: p.
Includes index.
1. Public relations.   2. Entrepreneur.
3. New business enterprises.   I. Title.
HD59.S63   1986   659.2   86-4931
ISBN 0-917253-35-3

Library of Congress Catalog Card No. 86-4931

Printed in the United States of America

1 2 3 4 5 6 7 8 9 0

CONTENTS

PREFACE

Some years ago, I climbed the fence that separates the world of the mass media from the relatively new profession of public relations. However, as I strove to prepare myself for a new career, I encountered a dearth of information of the "nuts and bolts" variety. Public relations often was presented in such a manner that the discipline seemed remote, abstract, and unrelated to the real world.

And the information which was available always raised the question of whether the writer ever had set foot in a newsroom. I also realized that I had something to offer to the profession.

Public Relations for the Entrepreneur and the Growing Business covers the little things which may not appear in a publication of a theoretical nature. They include when and when not to approach a media representative, how to set up a picture and how to improve delivery in a speaking engagement. It also removes the mystique from public relations and presents the profession to the reader in simple, down-to-earth terms.

The book is a practical, how-to-do-it guide for owners and managers of new or expanding businesses who want to know how to handle their own public relations work. It does not call for expensive specialists to create favorable images for their firms and products. The book lays out simple guidelines, asking for no more than a willingness to work and awareness that much of public relations is pure common sense.

To provide an in depth understanding of public relations, the book explores its function as a marketing tool and clarifies its relationship with advertising. The many facets of public relations are outlined in the ensuing chapters to emphasize the fact that the profession is much more than a program to pump out news releases for the media. And numerous examples of my personal experiences and those of others strengthen these points.

Public Relations for the Entrepreneur and the Growing Business also discusses the advantages of internal and external execution, how to choose and monitor an outside agency, outlines the process of writing news releases, shows how to get along with the media, provides tips for photography, and explains how to stage successful news conferences, media events, open houses and exhibits. It covers the advantages of building good community relations and the public relations value of affirmative action programs, speaking engagements, and writing articles and books. If you and your company suddenly are confronted with an emergency situation, this book will help you prepare for it in advance to keep damage to a minimum and cope with other PR problems.

No modern book on public relations would be complete without a chapter on methods of measuring the impact of your efforts on the public as well as your output. I have such a chapter on how to sample public opinion.

Finally, I would like to thank the people who helped to make this book possible. I am indebted to Dr. Thomas A. Easton for his expert guidance and inspiration. Ron Palmquist and David Ferguson generously shared their time with me. And to my wife, Mignon, son, Steven, and daughter, Kay, I appreciate their loving patience and moral support.

Norman R. Soderberg

CHAPTER

1

1

The Function of Public Relations

To expand your markets and fatten your bottom line, you must reach your customers. That is, you must be sure that everyone who might possibly be interested in your product or service knows about it.

But that is only half of your marketing campaign. If it were the whole, advertisements, commercials, and direct mailings could do the job. If they were all you needed, this book would be a very different thing.

The second half of your marketing campaign is making sure that while your potential customers know about your product or service, they also *think favorably of it*. To accomplish this, you need to do all you can to build a positive image for your company and whatever you sell. This is the function of public relations.

The key to effective public relations is very simple: *Do good work, and call attention to it.* There is more to public relations as well, of course, but this is the key. The sequence is crucial. Do the good work *first*, then

3

call attention to it. Do not call attention to your work *before* you do it, for it may not live up to your promises.

Do you need another warning? Do not rely on gimmicks. Leave the hot air balloons, dancing girls, and dignitaries to the circus. Your cause advances more surely if you stress *substance*, not puff.

INCREASING PROFITS

Speaking of substances, there is probably none more thoroughly familiar to the American mind than the hamburger. In 1955, Ray Kroc took that traditional bun-enclosed patty and set in motion the events which led to one of the greatest marketing coups of the century. In bygone days, the establishment in which you purchased a hamburger was usually not the cleanest place in the world. These "hamburger joints" catered to teenage crowds and definitely were not family-oriented.

After Kroc approached Richard and Maurice McDonald, owners of a small hamburger restaurant, the three started the well-known McDonald's franchise chain. There was no magic formula for the success of the operation. Their secret was simple: give the customers what they want. Using public relations as a marketing tool, McDonald's offered fast, efficient and courteous service in a clean and pleasant setting. The firm created a family atmosphere by installing exotic playground equipment, giving away small, inexpensive children's games and toys such as balloons, presenting awards to athletes in neighboring high schools and colleges, and staging birthday parties. The chain also created a character, Ronald McDonald, who has become almost as famous as Santa Claus among the younger set.

McDonald's met the needs of the consumer by carefully choosing locations and franchise operators. It gave the operators excellent management training at a central facility and supported them with high-quality, high-powered promotion programs. Did the public relations campaign increase profits for McDonald's? After 30 years, the firm is a multibillion-dollar operation and has captured 20 percent of the fast food market.

EMPTY PROMISES

Suppose, by some quirk of fate, that McDonald's high-powered, high-quality promotion campaign had preceded the construction of its restaurants or that the establishments had failed to live up to its promise. People would have found just another dirty, greasy hamburger joint or a hole in the wall. Their disappointment would have kept them away in droves. The public relations would have done more harm than good.

MARKETING CONCEPT

The McDonald's story is a classic example of what William A. Cohen and Marshall E. Reddick (1981) describe as the "marketing concept." The first principle, consumer orientation or giving the customers what they want, was followed religiously by the fast-food chain. To achieve consumer orientation, you look to the needs and desires of the customer instead of your own. McDonald's did not simply try to sell hamburgers. The chain examined the market, determined what that market wanted, and then developed its business around this want.

COORDINATING EFFORT

The second principle of the marketing concept involves the coordination and integration of corporate efforts. All members of the McDonald's family, from the franchisees to the kids behind the counters, were thoroughly trained in the techniques of providing fast, efficient, courteous service and clean facilities. Each member of the staff learned exact duties and carried them out with precision.

PROFIT ORIENTATION

Let's not be coy about it. The reason for public relations is money. It puts dollars into the pocket of the small business person when the public is convinced that his or her product, company, personnel and service are the best. And, when the small business owner prospers, so does the country as a whole. Even though your emphasis is on satisfying customer needs and wants, you must still make a reasonable profit. Profit orientation is the third principle in the marketing concept. The McDonald's success story reflects this strategy of offering a quality product at a reasonable price.

MARKETING AND PUBLIC RELATIONS

You may have noticed, at this point, that I have used the terms marketing and public relations interchangeably. That is because public relations is a marketing tool and definitely belongs in the marketing department of a business. Marketing is the aggregate of functions involved in moving goods from the producer to the consumer. Public relations is one of the functions necessary to generate good will and understanding for the business. The McDonald's fast-food chain would never have been able to achieve its marketing coup without public relations, and public relations, by itself, would have been useless without the goals and disciplines laid out in the marketing concept.

KINDS OF PUBLIC RELATIONS

Are you the owner or manager of an expanding business which you hope will someday reach the magnitude of the McDonald's empire? The fact that you have taken the initiative to acquire this book indicates you are on the right track and are determined to build a positive image for your company. But the second step may require more thought and planning. If you own a fast-food chain like McDonald's, you may want to emphasize quick, efficient, courteous service in a clean and pleasant setting.

If your firm manufactures a precision product, you may want to stress that yours is the best on the market. Don't be afraid to give examples of how your product is being used to expand new frontiers. Show how your gidget is used in the Space Shuttle.

Maybe your company deals with a natural resource such as oil, coal, lumber, or copper. Because of environmental considerations, you begin with the disadvantage of a built-in negative image. You've got a greater challenge than the McDonald's chain (almost everybody likes hamburgers). You've got to show the public that your industry is a friend of the environment. One magazine advertisement sponsored by the oil industry pictures a school of fish congregating around a Texas oil tower. The message suggests that the tower's construction has improved the fishing.

If your company offers a service to the public, you may want to hang your public relations campaign on the quality of that service. In the event that your company, like McDonald's, features both a product and a service, you may decide to give a plug to all phases of your operation.

If you offer specialized services, you may want to emphasize very specific areas. For example, executive training agencies like to show prospective students that their instructors are better educated, their courses provide better training, and their graduates quickly move up the ladder of success. These agencies also emphasize the expensive equipment in their computer centers.

Can you stand still more advice? Don't get carried away with your public relations spiel. When you say that your computer equipment is more sophisticated and your courses are better than in other agencies, make sure it is true. Prospective students aren't stupid. If they have reached a level of intelligence that qualifies them for executive training, they have a pretty good idea about the programs and equipment at other agencies. Be honest with them. If the information about one aspect of your program is less than accurate, you may find your agency losing credibility on all fronts.

Peruse the written material from other agencies or telephone them to compare the quality of their programs with yours. Executive training agencies are more than anxious to discuss their programs with anyone who calls.

Suppose your organization is a magazine which depends on subscriptions for success. In that case, it would be well to prime your PR campaign to focus on the benefits of being a subscriber. Perhaps you may want to show your target audience how the magazine improved the life of one subscriber by encouraging him to return to college and pursue a successful career. And give concrete examples of how the magazine helped his ability to think for himself by reading about the experiences of others.

BUILDING UP THE BOSS

One of the most important and challenging chores for your PR person is building up the boss. If you, as head of the company, are doing the public relations, then you might take an objective look at yourself. The boss may be the company's chief executive officer (CEO), the president, a partner or simply the owner. And the boss may be a wimp. But that is where the challenge comes in.

In order to project the best possible image of the boss to the public, you've got to capitalize on strong points. At the risk of becoming too preachy, I would advise you not to book him for the keynote speech at the annual meeting of the Chamber of Commerce, or for appearances on radio or television talk shows, if he does not speak comfortably in public or if poise and confidence are lacking. It can do more harm than good.

Remember, people identify personal appearance, presence of mind and confidence with the quality of your company's product or service. The person may be a mental giant in the field, but if the boss doesn't come across well in a personal appearance, you would do well to consider another means of gaining exposure. The person who represents your company in public should be able to think on his feet, be reasonably well groomed, and project a vibrant image.

There are other ways, too, of generating respect and prestige for the boss — and the company — if she doesn't fit that personality mold. Analyze her. What are her hobbies, skills, interests, and past achievements? Concentrate on the print media. Maybe she raises prize African violets in her spare time. She may hit the horse show circuit every weekend with a stable of fine Arabian steeds. Both are good possibilities for newspaper feature stories or articles in the horticultural and horsy magazines.

Or he may hold a Bronze Star medal earned in battle during World War II. How about a story in the *American Legion Magazine?* What would be better on the VE Day anniversary issue of the local paper than a write-up on the personal experiences of your veteran of the Normandy invasion?

There are other avenues in which your company's boss can put his best foot forward. He should be a joiner. The Rotary, Kiwanis, and Lions Clubs, the American Legion, VFW, the Masons, Knights of Columbus, B'nai B'rith and the Chamber of Commerce might have his name on their membership rolls. He should be active and hold office in these organizations. Every time he does good things and his name appears in the newspaper identifying him as the president of the Imperial Machine Co., the firm will get a boost. True, active membership in community and civic organizations demands time, but with a little planning and delegation of responsibility, it can be done. If he doesn't want to become a joiner, maybe he isn't the right person to head the Imperial Machine Co. When you find out how to tell him so and retain your job, you will be a PR person.

TARGETING YOUR PR

You wouldn't try to sell a baby carriage to a golden ager, a lawn mower to someone living in a city apartment, or a boat to a nomad in the Sahara Desert, yet many new products fail every day because of just that type of marketing error. When Ray Kroc created his McDonald's fast-food empire, he meticulously embraced the marketing concept principle of giving the consumer what he wants. Efficient and courteous service in a clean and pleasant setting was exactly what the public was looking for, a fact demonstrated by his obvious success.

The marketing concept has changed from the early *production-oriented* period, when goods were so scarce that consumers bought whatever was available, to the *sales-oriented period*, marked by high-pressure, hard-sell approaches, to today, the *consumer-oriented period*, when marketers try very hard to respond to consumer needs.

William Rudelius, W. Bruce Erickson and William J. Bakula, Jr., (1976) note that two steps are essential to a successful marketing program:

1. Identifying the target market, the specific groups of customers to whom the company wishes to appeal with its products or services.

2. Selecting the appropriate blend of marketing activities, the kind and amount of activities necessary to reach the target market.

Public relations is a marketing tool. That is, we implement the marketing concept by means of public relations through the paid advertisement, the news release, photography, the speaker's podium, the billboard, word-of-mouth, direct mailings and a multitude of other methods devised by the creativity of the practitioner. And every one of these tools requires careful targeting.

ADVANCE PLANNING

We begin the targeting by advance planning. You will save a lot of time if you make certain decisions before launching your PR campaign. For example, do you want local, regional, or national publicity? If you're publicizing a nationwide chain like McDonald's, I'm sure you want a little of each. You compete with other fast-food establishments on the community level and you want to draw customers from the region and beyond.

Yet, for a ski resort, there wouldn't be much point in local advertising. Chances are your ski center is the only one in the area and everyone in town knows about it. If they haven't used it already, they probably never will. The same would go for the Imperial Machine Co., which makes precision devices for fire engine pumpers. Every community has a fire department and the firm would want to tout its product in trade journals throughout the country. And again, probably half of the local fire department works at the Imperial Machine Co. So what would be the sense of advertising the product on a local level?

On the other hand, Pete's Delicatessen wouldn't be likely to draw patronage from outside the community even though it is known for fine prepared foods such as cooked meats, preserves, salads, and relishes. Every community has its own delicatessen. Pete would do well to limit his advertising to the local newspaper, local radio station and word-of-mouth. The same advertising strategy would apply to the local movie theater. When virtually every community has its own cinema center, it would be a waste of money to try to attract patronage from outside the region.

To backtrack a bit, let's make sure the meaning of the term *target market* is, to borrow a phrase often used by a former president, "crystal clear" in our minds. Your target market could be any segment of society with a particular set of characteristics. These could include age, sex, social status, educational level, marital status, nationality, religion, interests, geographic distribution, profession, occupation, skills, hobbies, or entertainment preferences. The examples are endless. And the more specific the target market, the better chance of success for the product or service. For example, the college student would be a good target market for a quality calculator. However, wouldn't the college student who majors in accounting be a better target market for the calculator than the one who majors in history?

Once the target market is identified, we need to define the *marketing mix* to ensure the success of the market or service. First, we must develop the right product or service for the particular target market we have in mind. Second, we must select the appropriate channels of distribution to be sure that the product reaches the target market at the right time and in the right place. These channels could include retailing and wholesaling organizations. Third, we must set a reasonable price that provides good value to the customer and adequate revenue to the producer. At this point, we as PR people are ready to do our thing. Through sales, advertising, and other means, we communicate information about the product or service to the consumer.

IDENTIFYING THE TARGET MARKET

We now have a pretty good idea of the meaning of the term *target market*. But how do we identify our target market? Much of the identification procedure is simple common sense. It doesn't take a great deal of thought to realize that St. Petersburg, Florida with its high percentage of retired persons would not be a good location to concentrate our baby carriage sales campaign. San Diego, California, with a great many young persons would be much better. However, in some cases, it might take a more sophisticated process to pinpoint the target market.

The marketing specialists have a little device they call the *market grid* to help select their target markets. E.

Jerome McCarthy (1975) points out that when a market-oriented person examines potential target markets, he is aware that what is often considered as one market may actually be many smaller, more homogeneous markets. That is why we employ the analytical approach to market segmentation. The market grid is a chart set up to show relevant market characteristics. Each square in the chart represents a smaller, more homogeneous market.

Figure 1-1. Market Grid for Air Conditioning

Region / Place of Use	North-east	Southeast	Mid-west	Southwest	North-west
Home					
Commercial Buildings		✕			
Schools					
Hospitals					
Government Buildings					
Farm Buildings					
Other Buildings					

The simple market grid in Figure 1-1 could be used to determine the target market for air conditioners. Drawn purely for illustrative purposes, it may not reflect the true market. Nevertheless, the example would indicate that commercial buildings in the Southeast are the target market for air conditioning. However, let me reiterate my previous statement that what is often considered as one market may actually be many smaller, more homogeneous markets.

In other words, commercial buildings in the Southeast could be broken down into smaller target markets. These variations, often called *customer dimen-*

sions, could include the type of commercial activity, the size and scope of the operation, gross sales, number of employees, size of physical plant, and others. For example, some commercial operations are heavily computerized and require more air conditioners to maintain constant environmental conditions. The region also could be broken down into high-density areas, mountainous areas, and other factors which might affect the need for air conditioning. Lest you believe that we strayed too far afield in our pursuit of clarity, let me emphasize that the identification of the market was necessary in order to provide a target for our public relations.

THE MARKETING MIX

To achieve success in marketing our product or service, it would be good to follow the example of Howard D. Johnson in his development of America's first franchise restaurant chain. As we have already discussed briefly, marketing specialists follow a definite procedure in developing the marketing mix. They pinpoint four basic variables called *four P's:* Product, Place, Promotion, and Price. It goes without saying that Howard Johnson had the right *product* when he formed his marketing strategy. He really couldn't go wrong with ice cream. Almost everybody likes it. He certainly satisfied the needs of the customers.

FRANCHISING IS KEY!

The value of a product or service is determined by its availability when and where it is needed. Goods and services do not flow automatically from the producer to the consumer. By 1940, Howard Johnson had his name on 135 company-owned and franchised restaurants along the East coast. Most were located on major highways. He was successful in getting the right product to the target market by means of the right *place.* Although the chain eventually included motels, an institutional catering service, and food processing plants as well as restaurants, the name Howard Johnson continued to be closely associated with ice cream and the famous "28 flavors." The entrepreneur capitalized on the excellent reputation of his ice cream.

Promotions, the third *P*, includes personal selling, mass selling, and sales promotion and is concerned with any method that communicates to the target market about the right product to be sold in the right place at the right price. Personal selling, direct face-to-face relationships between sellers and potential customers, added much to the success of the Howard Johnson enterprise. The customers were attracted by the bright orange roofs on the restaurants along major highways and the courteous and efficient service within.

The Howard Johnson success story reflects the strategy of offering a quality product at a reasonable *price*. There are many factors in the process of deciding the right price to complete the marketing mix. They include competition in the target market, existing practices on markups, discounts, terms of sale, and legal restrictions.

GOOD WILL

What is the value of good will? For some businesses, it may be more important than for others. Good will, the end result of public relations, may be measured for accounting purposes by what a business earns beyond the average earnings of similarly situated businesses. It may be due partly to the advantages of location, or, in the case of a personal service business, to the personality of the owner. Generally, however, it may be linked to the character of the business, which was built by fair dealing and a sound public relations policy.

In one case, a small but nationally known manufacturing plant burned to the ground. The plant, equipment, inventories of raw materials, and company records were a complete loss. The firm had some insurance but not nearly enough to finance the cost of putting the business in operation again. Yet, the owners had earned an excellent reputation for honesty over the years. They had paid their bills promptly, treated employees well and earned the respect of employees, suppliers, customers, and the local newspaper. The local bankers floated a stock issue and it was quickly oversubscribed. Within a few weeks, equipment was obtained, a temporary building was erected and the company was back in operation again. With nothing more than good will, the firm was able to resume its business. Good will proved to be its most valuable asset. Because of its intangible nature, accountants hesitate to place this product of favorable public opinion on balance sheets, however. Many businesses have been sold at 10 to 20 times their net worth because of good will.

BUSINESS SUCCESS THROUGH PR

Remember the marketing principle, "give the customers what they want," that has been the key to success for so many franchise operations? Joseph J. and Suzy Fucini (1985) cite the stories of many other business persons who have used that same formula in their climb up that ladder of entrepreneurial success.

Take the example of Joyce C. Hall who founded Hallmark Cards in the early part of this century. Most of the greeting cards sold in the United States at that time were imported from England and Germany. They were elaborately engraved and made for only two occasions, Christmas and Valentine's Day. Hall felt that Americans would prefer more informal cards that could be sent more often. He formed the idea of colorful illustrated cards with upbeat verses expressing sentiments like friendship, congratulations, and sympathy. His first card, in 1916, was an immediate success, and by the early 1920s, his cards were being sold in stores throughout the East and Midwest. In 1923, he extended his name into the word *Hallmark* to create an identifiable brand name suggestive of the highest quality. As the years went by, the greeting card pioneer found many ways to project this image. He coined the advertising slogan, "When you care enough to send the very best," used well-known artists and writers, the company's most effective public relations, and sponsored the "Hallmark Hall of Fame" TV show in the 1950s and 1960s. Until his retirement in 1966, Hall followed a policy of personally clearing every single Hallmark illustration and verse. The founder of Hallmark Cards had the uncanny ability of knowing exactly what the public wanted, a talent to which his artists and writers will attest. The company was publishing 8 million greeting cards a day when Hall died in 1982.

LANE BRYANT APPAREL

Another entrepreneur who knew how to give the customers what they want was Lane Bryant, a Lithuanian-born seamstress who developed a reputation for designing clothes that flattered the wearer's figure and eventually built a $50 million business.

Lane Bryant's clientele grew steadily as her designing skill became known in New York City. She was asked by a pregnant customer to make something practical as well as pretty so she could continue an active social life. At that time, pregnant women were expected to stay at home. There was no such thing as maternity clothes for street wear. The seamstress became a pioneer in that field. She designed a comfortable and concealing maternity gown by attaching a bodice to an accordion-pleated skirt with an elastic band that would expand with a woman's waist. The customer was excited with the creation and recommended Lane Bryant to her friends. Soon Bryant was receiving orders from pregnant women throughout the city.

Lane Bryant decided in 1910 to specialize in ready-to-wear maternity fashions. She had already gained a great deal of public relations through that valuable medium of word-of-mouth. However, when she tried to gain further publicity for her stylish collection of dresses for mothers-to-be, most newspapers' Victorian standards caused them to refuse to accept advertising for a product as suggestive as maternity wear. Finally, *The New York Herald* agreed to place an ad which, among other claims, asserted, "It is no longer the fashion nor the practice for expectant mothers to stay in seclusion. Doctors, nurses and psychologists agree that at this time a woman should think and live as normally as possible. To do this, she must go out among other people, she must look like other people." The advertisement was an immediate success. Soon Lane Bryant was filling orders from mothers-to-be throughout the United States by means of a catalog that showed 32 pages of maternity street dresses.

Eventually the firm added fashionable dresses for overweight and large proportioned women to its line. Like maternity wear, the revolutionary apparel was promoted in high-pressure magazine ads. Again she was highly successful in this new venture. The designer continued to expand with branch stores in eight cities besides Manhattan with full lines of wardrobe accessories for stout customers and new categories for tall women and chubby teenage girls.

HONDA MOTORCYCLES

I can remember when one thought a motorcyclist had to be a long-haired, bearded and broad-shouldered tough perched on a two-wheeled machine. He would be wearing a Nazi helmet, a leather vest, combat boots, and tight-fitting pants. An Iron Cross would hang at his bare chest. The word "Mom" would be tattooed on his biceps.

Today that particular image is not quite so sharp. Motorcyclists are students, young mothers, commuters, retired grocers, even grandmothers. That is quite an image reversal. In fact, it smacks of the same public relations stuff as Ray Kroc's marketing coup which shook the hamburger industry out of dirty, greasy "joints" and into pleasant, family-oriented settings. The man responsible for bringing the first socially acceptable motorcycle to middle-class America in the early 1960s was Soichiro Honda, a Japanese blacksmith's son.

He began making motorcycles in 1948 in a small workshop near his home. His business began to boom in 1958 when he introduced a new lightweight vehicle called the Super Cub. It combined the durability of a large motorcycle with the economy and handling of a motor scooter. Two years later he built the largest motorcycle factory in the world at Suzuka.

But he had some public relations groundwork to do first. It would be necessary to change the tough-guy label connected with motorcycles. Honda felt it would be better to upgrade the general image of motorcycling rather than concentrate on the specific merits of his product. He was right.

If I might pause a moment to make a point, I would like to remind the reader that Honda observed one of the basic principles of public relations. *He did his good work first before calling attention to it.*

In 1962, Honda ran a national magazine advertisement built around the slogan, "You Meet the Nicest People on a Honda." The ad, designed by Grey Advertising of Los Angeles, depicted lively, cheerful illustrations of respectable Americans from all walks of life happily riding a Honda Super Cub. The ad was published in *Time, Life, Look* and other prominent, general-interest publications where it would be viewed by millions of readers who had never ridden a motorcycle. The ad was the forerunner of many which would repeat the same message: motorcycling could be clean, wholesome fun when it involved a quiet little machine like the Super Cub.

The public's attitude toward motorcycling changed almost overnight. Instead of regarding two-wheelers as vehicles strictly for black-leather-jacket toughs, Americans viewed motorcycling in a respectable new light. Honda then expanded his advertising campaign in 1963 to include television. The company purchased a one-quarter sponsorship of the Academy Awards telecast the following year. The day after the broadcast of the Oscar ceremonies, customer traffic at Honda showrooms reached an all-time high.

Within six years of launching his first "Nicest People" ad, Honda reported its one-millionth motorcycle sale in the United States. The company entered the automobile industry in 1963, and a few years later, Honda established itself as one of the world's major automobile manufacturers. When Honda retired as president of the firm in 1973, the company claimed an impressive 46 percent share of the American motorcycle market.

HEINZ KETCHUP

If anyone used gimmicks in his public relations or marketing campaign, it was Henry J. Heinz. But he didn't rely on gimmicks alone. His "57 Varieties," one of the greatest numerical slogans of all time, stressed substance as well as puff. His company already was producing more than 60 different kinds of pickles, relishes, and vinegar. However, Heinz selected number 57 for his slogan because he liked the way it looked. The entrepreneur exhibited the 57 Varieties monogram on 400 yellow rail-freight cars owned by his firm, in street cars throughout the United States, and in many other conspicuous places in the country. The signs have been a major factor in the success of the H.J. Heinz Co.

Heinz was one of the first advertisers to use an outdoor electric sign. He erected a six-story billboard showing a 40-foot pickle and 1,200 light bulbs at Fifth Avenue and 23rd Street in New York City. Heinz traveled widely and accumulated a massive collection of artifacts. Recognizing the public relations value of these items, he exhibited some of his more interesting artifacts in the Heinz Ocean Pier, an Atlantic City pavilion. The pier was his most ambitious promotional venture. It featured a large green pickle on each side of the entrance and a giant "57" sign. The exhibit attracted 15,000 persons a season and remained in operation until 1944 when it was closed because of hurricane damage.

By 1896, Heinz was a multimillionaire known nationally as the "Pickle King." A master at creating promotional gimmicks to generate publicity for his products, Heinz built up strong consumer recognition for the Heinz label at a time when bottled and canned foods were just beginning to be marketed under brand names. His talent in this area was considered a major reason for the phenomenal growth of the company. But, again, Heinz had quality products to back up his efforts.

As I have said before, Heinz did not base his promotional campaign on gimmicks alone. One of his most effective innovations was giving guided tours of his state-of-the-art industrial complex. About 20,000 visitors a year viewed Heinz's then-unheard-of fringe benefits, including an indoor gymnasium and swimming pool, a restaurant, and a fully-equipped hospital for the employees. Another feature of the plant which drew national attention was a turreted, three-story stable where the Heinz delivery horses were fed, watered, and brushed by electrically-operated machinery.

POSTUM, POST CEREALS

While Henry Heinz conducted his public relations program with big signs and exotic displays, Charles W. Post preferred to spread his message through smaller versions of the printed word. In 1895, Post decided to market Postum, a coffee substitute. He borrowed money to purchase advertisements in *Scribner's, Harpers Weekly* and other national publications. Post, who had a great deal of talent with words, wrote his own advertising copy. He literally frightened coffee drinkers into switching to Postum with claims that the caffeinated beverage caused rheumatism, heart disease, blindness, cowardliness, laziness, diminished mental capacity, and other maladies. Highly successful in his Postum campaign, Post then turned to a precooked cereal called Grape Nuts which he again touted with his flamboyant advertising practices. The entrepreneur introduced Grape Nuts as a builder of red blood cells, brain cells, and steady nerves, and a preventer of malaria, consumption and appendicitus in his magazine and newspaper ads.

Some publishers and the medical community criticized Post for his reckless advertising. It is no wonder. Most of the better publications of today would not accept advertisements with such outlandish claims. However, it is interesting to note that about the same period that the media accepted Post's irresponsible advertising, Lane Bryant encountered problems in trying to place newspaper ads for maternity wear. That type of hypocrisy in advertising policy may still exist today to some degree. The major TV networks, rife with sexual innuendo in their program content, recently rejected advertisements for contraceptives.

LIPTON TEA

When you set out to persuade Americans to switch from coffee to tea, you've got a job as formidable as convincing people of the respectability of hamburgers and motorcycles. Yet, Thomas J. Lipton tackled that problem with the same stubborn determination as that shown by Ray Kroc in the development of his fast-food empire and Soichiro Honda in his crusade to create a new image in the United States for two-wheeled vehicles.

A wealthy Scottish businessman, Lipton vowed to promote his favorite beverage on this side of the Atlantic after he ordered tea in a Chicago restaurant and was told, "Sorry, mister, we don't carry that stuff." He owned several tea plantations in Sri Lanka and was a major supplier of the drink in Europe.

Lipton came to this country as a young man, acquired a knowledge of slick window displays and clever advertisements as assistant manager of a large Manhattan grocery store, and returned to Glasgow in 1869 to apply those merchandising principles to his parents' struggling grocery. His promotional efforts included posters, a pair of large pigs called "Lipton's Orphans," dropping leaflets from hot air balloons, large window sculptures made from butter and sausage, and the "world's largest cheese" filled with gold coins.

If I might again issue a note of warning to business people, I would like to emphasize that Lipton, like Ray Kroc and Henry Heinz, had the quality products to support his advertising program. And, at the risk of sounding like a broken record, I would like to remind you that they did not rely on promotional gimmicks alone.

Flamboyant advertising stunts such as the circulation of leaflets from hot air balloons and "orphaned" pigs would not be used today by the average family grocery store, largely because of economic limitations. Of course, Lipton did not have mass media such as television or radio at his disposal. Today's grocer concentrates on newspaper and radio ads, newspaper supplements, trading stamps, coupons, and promotional prizes. However, in the tradition of Thomas Lipton, he might employ catchy window displays.

Lipton was a millionaire long before he became associated with his namesake tea. He became involved with tea in 1888 when he introduced several innovations such as eliminating the middleman, blending his own tea, and prepackaging. Lipton soon was selling the beverage to stores and restaurants throughout Europe.

In 1890, the entrepreneur was in the United States to gather information about the tea market and found it to be overpriced, inferior in quality, and lacking in freshness because of improper storage. Determined to persuade Americans to like tea, Lipton launched a massive campaign to give the beverage a new image in the United States. He inserted advertisements in newspapers to educate the public about tea and hired salesmen to introduce his product to hotels and restaurants. Lipton also gained much publicity for tea in 1893 when he persuaded the nation of Sri Lanka, a major producer of tea leaves, to operate a booth at the Chicago Exposition.

As I have previously stated, people identify a company's product or service with the person who represents the firm. The public's fascination with Thomas Lipton himself was probably the major factor in the promotion of tea in America. Tall, blue-eyed, and ruddy-cheeked, the millionaire Scotsman was well known both here and in Europe for his association with European royalty and his yacht-racing activities. With his *Shamrock* yachts, he competed five times in the prestigious America's Cup races about the turn of the century. Although he never was victorious in the contest, his gentlemanly sportsmanship continued to charm Americans.

BUDWEISER BEER

Another entrepreneur who sold his product by selling himself was Adolphus Busch, who became a junior partner in a struggling brewery owned by his father-in-law, Eberhard Anheuser, in 1865. Busch proved to be a spectacular salesman and, almost immediately, launched the St. Louis firm on the road to success. And he sold himself as aggressively as he sold his product. A personable, robust young man with a flowing mustache and a commanding voice, Busch developed friendship with tavern owners and beverage merchants. He also designed a "calling card" in the form of a jackknife with the E. Anheuser & Co. logo to make himself stand out among the dozens of other beer salesmen in the city. The knife contained a peephole through which could be viewed a picture of Adolphus Busch himself.

Busch cultivated the consumers as well as the retailers. He bought a fleet of impressive delivery wagons and high-stepping show horses and also became the first beer producer in the city to offer guided tours to the public through a remodeled brewing plant. Eventually, Busch's promotional efforts elevated the company to the level of leading breweries in St. Louis.

Let us now pause a moment to reflect on Busch's success and analyze his promotional techniques. As I have repeated on several occasions, do not rely on promotional gimmicks alone. Busch had gone about as far as he could with a beer of average quality. Now it was time to upgrade the product. In 1876, the super salesman unveiled a premium beverage now called Budweiser. Besides its extraordinary smoothness and taste, the beer had the additional advantage of retaining its flavor for long periods if pasteurized and bottled. This provided the opportunity to extend the market well beyond St. Louis and establish one of America's first national brands of beer.

Busch continued to sell his personality in the nationwide Budweiser campaign. He visited cities to introduce his premium beer, hosted lavish banquets, and continued to distribute an assortment of novelty items to keep the Budweiser name in front of tavern owners and customers.

In keeping with good public relations practices, Busch also continued his striving for quality instead of relying on promotional gimmicks alone. After the success of Budweiser, he marketed a draft beer in 1896 which was targetted for the very top of the American market. The super-premium beer, Michelob, was available only in draft form until it was sold in bottles and cans in 1961. To provide an entry in the popularly-priced segment of the market, a beer bearing the entrepreneur's namesake Busch label was introduced in 1955.

When Budweiser's 25th anniversary was celebrated in 1901, the Anheuser-Busch brewery had become the largest beer company in the world. Adolphus

Busch, one of the country's richest men at that time, left behind a personal fortune of $60 million when he died a few years later.

WHAT WILL YOU DO?

The last century's entrepreneurs have ridden a number of public relations and marketing techniques to success. Some of these techniques are unacceptable by present-day standards. Others remain in general use.

Among the most objectionable techniques are scare tactics such as Charles W. Post used in his marketing of the coffee substitute, Postum. He frightened coffee drinkers into switching to Postum with claims that it caused rheumatism, heart disease, blindness, cowardliness, laziness, diminished mental capacity, and other maladies.

However, many entrepreneurs of bygone days found success through methods which have become modern-day marketing concepts. Those who made their fortunes by giving the customers what they want include Joyce C. Hall of Hallmark Cards, Lane Bryant with her special-size fashions for women, Soichiro Honda and his Super Cub motorcycle, Henry J. Heinz with his "57 Varieties", Ray Kroc with his McDonald's fast-food empire, and Adolphus Busch with the beer industry.

Others made inroads in the business field by identifying their vibrant personalities with their products. Among them were Thomas Lipton with his tea empire and Adolphus Busch.

If you are seeking a common denominator for entrepreneurial success, however, one factor stands head and shoulders above the others. These business persons *always did the good work first before calling attention to it.* And they continually upgraded the quality of their product or service.

Now the ball is in your hands and it is time for your firm to run with it. As the owner of your company, it is up to you to decide the next move. There are several alternatives. You may want to pass it to an outside public relations agency, hand it off to a marketing manager or public relations director within the company, or run with it yourself. The following chapter will provide the information you need to make a decision on who will do the public relations for your company.

CHAPTER

2

2

The PR Executive

If you are the owner or president of a very small or newly-formed business with a limited PR budget, chances are you'll be doing your PR work yourself. In that case, this book is just what the doctor ordered. It will show you how to diagnose your PR needs, plan your campaign and implement it.

If your company is a little larger and you have a few bucks earmarked to spread good will for the firm, you might delegate the PR task to a marketing or public relations director. Or you might decide that it would be more cost-effective to engage an external public relations or advertising agency to enhance your firm's image. Again this book will show you how to select the right agency, get the most for your dollars, and monitor the PR operation.

Whatever you do, you are ultimately responsible for your public relations. If something goes wrong in your marketing campaign, you may set your marketing or PR director on the right track. But, you must take the ultimate blame. The buck stops with you.

31

THE PR PERSON

As head of your company, how do you select the person who will do the public relations? There is no such thing as an ideal PR person. The individual you have in mind may have skills in one area but not in another. It is rare indeed to find a super being who possesses expertise in advertising, speech services, maintaining archives, writing, communicating with the public, community relations, press, radio and television relations, audio-visuals, educational relations, research and information, graphic design, photographic services, and promotional techniques. The person may have excellent writing skills, but his speaking ability and personality may leave much to be desired. If the main thrust of your PR effort calls for speeches to various organizations, you might do well to consider another candidate for the job.

By the same token, if you want to advertise your product on TV, it might be a good idea to find someone with a background in television programming. Or, you may want a person who is good in the magazine advertising field.

You should also take a long, hard, objective look at yourself if you, as head of the company, plan to do the public relations. If you do not meet the criteria necessary for your firm's PR needs, it might be time to consider an outside agency.

QUALIFICATIONS OF THE PR EXECUTIVE

As I have previously emphasized, the qualifications of a PR person vary with the particular problems and firm with which he or she is associated. However, in virtually all cases, the position requires a creative and enterprising person with a knowledge of mass psychology and the mechanics of communication, good news judgment, and a good deal of common sense and sound judgment. The person also should make friends easily.

The one who continually changes jobs is not a good choice for a public relations executive. The man or woman should have a thorough and intimate knowledge of the problems of the business in order to effectively guide its public relations. The best way to get this knowledge is on the job.

The successful public relations person must by no means be an extreme, back-slapping extrovert with unlimited wit and a repertoire of jokes at his disposal. The entertainment field, especially films and television, has done a disservice to public relations people in portraying them as sleazy characters with a thousand questionable tricks and gimmicks. With the possible exception of the theater, the old concept that a public relations person is a glorified press agent is also becoming obsolete. However, the modern PR executive still should have a flair for the dramatic.

Public relations is a respectable and honorable profession with hard-working people interested in doing a good job. The PR practitioner must have a sincere desire to help people, take an interest in their problems, and be considerate of others in relations with reporters, broadcasters, associates, printers, and others with whom he comes in contact.

Many former newspaper reporters eventually wind up in the public relations field because the publicity function of PR work is so important. Although this does not necessarily mean that a good reporter would make a fine public relations person, there is much in common between the two professions. A reporter may learn to gather some kinds of news and how to write it correctly, but if he fails to discern the significance of a story and express it so others will understand it, his work will not influence public opinion despite its many good points. The quality that makes a good newspaper person must, in the opinion of the editors, exist in the beginning. He or she must be able to overcome public apathy and know how to appeal to the instincts that motivate people to action.

Technical knowledge gained from newspaper experience also is most valuable in public relations. If the PR person is responsible for a company publication or house organ, an understanding of headings, layouts, and what it takes to make a publication exciting and interesting will be helpful. That is where editorial experience on a newspaper or magazine is invaluable and why so many public relations people have come up through journalism. They know how to express themselves clearly and concisely.

Even though the public relations field is filled with former newspaper reporters, many of the top personnel have never worked for a newspaper, magazine, or any other publication. A great many have advertising backgrounds and their strength consists of developing opportunities in public relations.

DUTIES OF A PR PERSON

The PR executive is more than just a publicity agent. There is no question that publicity is an important part of the work. Some companies still measure the effectiveness of their PR campaigns by the number of times the name of their firm is mentioned by the media. However, the PR person has four basic responsibilities:

1. To interpret public opinion and advise management concerning matters involving a company's relations with the public;
2. To study various combinations of circumstances in connection with a firm's relations with the public, and to generate opportunities for gaining more public acceptance of its policies, products, and activities;
3. To disseminate good publicity about the company to the public;
4. To estimate the effect of the firm's PR on the public to determine if the effort has been worthwhile in terms of both money and time.

Journalism schools in many leading universities

offer public relations courses, which emphasize the measurement of public opinion and interpreting it to management as well as shaping the minds of the public.

FITTING THE PR PERSON TO THE JOB

In assigning a person to your company's PR duties, you may want to compile a checklist to choose the individual who best fits the job. You could take each candidate, list the strongest points of each, and proceed from there.

And don't forget yourself. Even though you may not be the person who implements the PR campaign, you, as head of the company, should monitor the program constantly and be familiar with its weaknesses as well as its strengths. Maybe you have a talent such as excellent speaking skills which could be used in the campaign. Who would be better than the president to carry the company's message to the public?

If you have a marketing director, include him or her in your deliberations. Public relations is a marketing tool and the PR person should report to or work closely with the marketing director.

If you have the "ideal" candidate on your check list, he or she has expertise or strong skills in the following areas:

1. Writing and editing.
2. The editorial and printing practices of newspapers and other periodicals.
3. Knowledge of the electronic media (radio and television).
4. Publicity, and a specialized knowledge of the field in which it is sought.
5. Public opinion polling.
6. Promotions.
7. Advertising.
8. Photography.
9. Graphic arts.

10. Marketing.
11. Speech services.
12. Research, information and the maintenance of archives.
13. Public communications.
14. Community relations.
15. Educational relations.
16. Teaching ability.
17. Analytical ability (public relations planning as compared to publicity alone).
18. Organizational ability.
19. Managerial ability.
20. Audio-visuals.

The ideal candidate also has the following traits:

1. Common sense.
2. Creativity.
3. News sense.
4. Interest in people.
5. Business sense.
6. Sincerity.
7. Charisma.
8. Dramatic sense.

Because public relations is such a broad field, the checklist of skills and traits could go on and on. As I have previously said, there is no such thing as an ideal PR person. If the individual you have in mind to do your company PR has a great many of the above skills, you have a gem. Don't let him or her get away.

In selecting your company PR person, you should consider several factors of course. Some jobs call for a lot of platform work while others require great writing and editorial skill. Still others emphasize teaching ability. When publicity is a main objective, the public relations executive should be a good salesperson because some editors are reluctant to use publicity releases.

The type of person who seems to do best in public relations work is quiet, sincere, honest, and straight-forward. With the entertainment field quite often portraying the PR person with the opposite traits, a person of integrity has a strong appeal in winning friends and influencing good will. He or she should be young enough to get around and do things and old and experienced enough to have good judgment. And the person should be in good health to stand up under the drive and work involved in public relations.

Some PR executives are more concerned with publicizing themselves than their firm. They spend much of their time entering contests and compiling scrapbooks. Most of the better PR people remain in the background and let someone else step into the spotlight, earning as a bonus more respect and cooperation from others in the company as a team worker. If you, as head of the business, are doing the public relations, this rule does not apply to you. People identify you with the quality of your company's product or service and you should take center stage with the best possible image you can project.

Your public relations person should remain in the background, but this does not mean becoming a hermit. The business of creating a favorable image for your company also involves participation in various civic and professional organizations. The person can make things happen without hogging the spotlight. The PR executive should meet people easily and get along well with them in their organizations. You don't want the sort of person who tries to dominate a discussion, but rather one who has the ability to contribute without being argumentative.

The importance of selecting a good manager for your PR operation cannot be overemphasized. The individual should be able to motivate people and stimulate them to the extent that they will cooperate and perform to their full capabilities.

In most expanding businesses, PR personnel must accomplish their goals and work within the confines of a limited budget. The person who handles your public relations must be adept at controlling expenditures. Some public relations executives think they have to establish a reputation as big spenders by lavishly entertaining people who may be in a position to do them some good, staging big press parties, purchasing tickets to dramatic productions and sporting events, and bestowing gifts. There is some evidence that this type of activity produces favorable results to a limited degree. However, it is not as necessary as is generally assumed, especially for expanding businesses. As far as gifts are concerned, one former newspaper colleague of mine always followed a simple rule: Never accept anything that cannot be consumed within a 24-hour period.

I can remember attending a number of lavish parties staged by General Dynamics/Electric Boat when I was a young reporter with *The Day* newspaper of New London, Connecticut. These events usually featured an open bar, gourmet food, and entertainment for members of the media in Southeastern Connecticut. There is no question that the parties were enjoyable. Yet, I cannot recall a single case in which my manner of approaching a story about Electric Boat was influenced by these parties. The firm eventually discontinued the parties. A good manager should know just how far to go with entertainment and gifts and constantly ask himself the question, "Does it justify the cost?"

THE ISOLATED PR PERSON

If you, as head of your business, do not plan to do the public relations yourself, the person who performs this task should be chosen from among the top management. He or she should have access to all policy-making meetings of the company officers, directors, trustees, and staff. The person who handles your PR is the connecting link or liaison between your company and the public. If that person does not know what is going on within the company, how can she convey the firm's message to the public? If you do not have confidence enough in the person to allow this kind of access, then, by all means, find a replacement.

I knew of one organization which treated its public relations director like a glorified secretary (not meant to slight the secretarial profession). The president was always "in conference" or "too busy" to talk to the PR director. When the PR person did get a chance to scale the ivory tower and speak to the president, his ideas usually were stonewalled. Although he was well qualified for the position, the president and other members of top management gave the PR director no opportunity to ply his profession.

When the president became aware of something he thought had PR value, he sent word to the PR person to write a news release without soliciting advice. Consequently, the public relations practitioner was forced to work within a vacuum. He knew little about the innermost operations of the organization. In fact, the top managers, who were distrustful of the media, thought they were indeed clever by their success in keeping information from the PR director.

Eventually, the bottom line began to shrink and they wondered why. In this case, the company had an image problem because the PR person did not have the needed authority and the full cooperation of top management. Even though the head of the organization did not serve as the practitioner, he badly needed education in the field of public relations so he could support his PR person.

A PR SURVEY

As one of the graduate school requirements for my master's degree, I prepared a thesis on *Public Relations Practices of Maine Mutual Savings Banks.* As of January 1, 1980, there were 29 savings banks in the State of Maine with 92 branches. The study was conducted by means of a mail survey questionnaire sent to the presidents of all 29 Maine savings banks.

Twenty-two of the banks with total assets ranging from less than $25 million to more than $100 million responded to the questionnaire. One item on the questionnaire sought information on the background of the person completing the survey form. Answering the question was optional, and 18 of the 22 respondents chose to answer at least parts of this section. Of those who answered the survey, 15 singled out the bank president as the person most involved in public relations. Three reported that the vice-president had the PR duties. Three more selected any bank officer who is available or the one most familiar with the subject of the public relations effort. One named the chief executive officer as the PR person at the bank. One bank delegated the PR responsibilities to the marketing officer. The survey indicated that in most Maine savings bank at least, the president did the PR chores.

However, despite my finding that mutual savings banks within the state of Maine are conducting an effective public relations campaign, the education and experience in the PR field of bank presidents has been sadly neglected. Eight of the 15 bank presidents who were most involved in the PR effort had no formal training in public relations, no previous experience in public relations before joining the bank, and no previous experience with the news or advertising media. Only one of the 15 presidents most involved in public relations at their banks had any formal public relations experience.

In banks where officers other than the president were most involved in public relations, those officers appeared to have a greater degree of training or experience in public relations and the media. Four had formal PR training, four had PR experience before joining the bank, and three had previous experience with the media. The survey would indicate that the head of an expanding business might do well to check his employees for expertise or experience in these areas before tackling the PR duties himself.

CHAPTER

3

3

Setting Up
Your PR Operation

Public relations is like happiness, true love, friendship, and apple pie. You can never get too much of it. But, a little bit of it is better than none at all. So you have to adjust and do the best you can within staffing and financial limitations.

A public relations operation can range from an owner of a small business conducting a one-person show to a massive PR department such as those of Ford Motor Company or Chrysler Corporation.

However, the owner or manager of a small expanding business and a competent secretary could set up an effective public relations program on a limited scale. A secretary would be necessary for the operation. With the owner dividing time between public relations and running the business, it would be impossible to implement the campaign. For example, the owner could write a news release and the secretary could type it in final form and mail it to the media. This avoids the extremely unproductive diversion of the owner from the business for clerical duties.

Care should be taken in the selection of your PR secretary. Choose someone with initiative who can take much of the load off your back with good ideas for efficient office procedure. He should answer the telephone in a professional manner and be a credit to your company. In public relations, that is the name of the game. Above all, a secretary with a good command of the English language would be a big plus for your firm.

Excellent oral and writing skills could supplement your efforts. A secretary who catches a costly error in a news release is worth his weight in gold. There is nothing worse than a communication with misspellings, poor grammar, and shoddy writing. People judge you and your company by the quality of your written messages. And, who knows, when your firm attains substantial growth and you decide to add a full-time PR person to your staff, he may be the ideal candidate for the position.

BASIC EQUIPMENT

In addition to the personnel, there are a few pieces of equipment which are essential to your PR operation. They include a good typewriter, a telephone and a photocopy machine. Of course there are many other items which will enhance the effectiveness of your operation. But those three will do for starters.

As far as typewriters are concerned, you can run the full gamut from the trusty manual, the electric, the IBM Memory to the word processor. Each has its own advantages. If you are from the old school and learned to type on a manual, chances are you will prefer to continue with a manual. You can pick up a used one at a very reasonable price. Want a few tips on where to get one? Most daily newspaper offices have computerized their operations within the last few years and reporters now file their copy on video display terminals (VDT's). If they still have a few old manuals laying around, they'd probably almost give them away. A business college or secretarial school in your area should have a few used ones knocking around. And your local dealer in business machines would be glad to give you some leads. She knows that, eventually, as your business grows, you will be buying new typewriters and other equipment from her. (If she is a successful business person, there is a good chance that she has acquired this PR know-how).

Let me give you a word of warning, however. Thoroughly check out any used typewriter that you purchase. Make sure the actions are good, all keys are working well, and the impressions are sharp and clear. There is nothing worse than a news release that looks like a chicken has walked across it after sloshing through a puddle of ink. Remember, in the best traditions of beer entrepreneur Adolphus Busch, the public (the media represent the public) judges you and your firm by the image you project.

If you can stand another word of advice, this is as good a time as any to give it. Change your typewriter ribbon often. Newspaper editors and TV and radio news directors get more news releases than they can use in the course of a day. If they have trouble reading one, it will almost certainly end up in the round file.

There is an advantage in working with a manual typewriter. If you start to write something and change your mind, you can pause with the keys halfway to the paper. With an electric machine, you can't do that. Once you touch the key, it's gone.

Electric typists also have their adherents. Like the manual, if you learned to type on the electric, that would be your choice. The electric typists say they get tired pounding on the keys of a manual. For a bit more money, you can probably find a used electric machine in the same places as the manual.

A memory typewriter is a much more sophisticated machine. But, if you can afford one, it is well worth the price. You will find it useful in direct mailings where you can retain the same body of the letter and personalize each heading. The carbon ribbon also makes an excellent impression for your news releases. As far as the word processor is concerned, it is an excellent instrument for all your needs. But you may want to wait until you are well established in business before tying up that much capital.

There is little to say about a telephone except to emphasize that if you are not adept at communicating with smoke signals, drums, or semaphore, it is an absolute must. In public relations, you take a great deal of information over the telephone. You may want to consider a telephone headset which frees your hands for typing. If you are not adept at shorthand, typing is easier than longhand note-taking.

Probably the largest capital outlay for your public relations operation is the photocopy machine. If you don't get a good one, it will nullify all your good work on the typewriter. If your business is not too far from a printing firm, you may want to have your work photocopied there in the beginning. However, sending your work out to be photocopied is only a temporary arrangement at best and you would do well to get your own machine as soon as possible. You might also look into the possibility of leasing one.

As your company expands, you may want to add photography to your PR operation. Portraits, generally known in journalism as one-column cuts or head shots, are much in demand by the print media with people stories. In fact, your story has a much better chance of being used if it is accompanied by a photograph. A picture with a story helps to draw the attention of a reader and lends itself to more prominent display by the publication.

You can begin modestly with a 35 mm single-lens reflex camera and an electronic flash attachment. A sheet stretched across a frame to provide a neutral background for head shots also is helpful. If you wish to further expand your photography operation, you may want to develop and print your own black and white film. More information about photography and darkroom equipment is included in Chapter 5.

THE BOOKSHELF

You can never get too much public relations. And many other items will increase the efficiency and quality of your operation. Probably the most important of these is a good dictionary; not the small pocket edition but a full-sized one. The dictionary should be in your reach as you write a news release. If you are not absolutely sure of the meaning or spelling of a word, you should use the dictionary. Remember, the public judges you and your company by the image you project. They will assume that your firm and your product is of the same quality as the news release. Some of the quality dictionaries are:

The American Heritage Dictionary of the English language

Webster's Ninth New Collegiate Dictionary

Oxford American Dictionary

The Random House College Dictionary

A Dictionary of Modern English Usage published by Oxford University Press

Funk & Wagnalls Standard Dictionary

You will also need media directories which contain such useful information as state-by-state listings of television and radio stations, daily and weekly newspapers, trade journals, other publications, editors, news directors, addresses, telephone numbers, circulation, policies, and styles. Some of them are:

The All-In-One Directory published by Gebbie Press, Box 1000 New Paltz, NY 12561.

Ayer Directory of Publications. Ayer Press, Bala Cynwyd, PA 19004.

Editor and Publisher Yearbook. 850 Third Ave., New York City 10022.

Broadcasting Yearbook. Broadcasting Publications, 1735 DeSales NW, Washington, D.C. 20036.

Writer's Market published by Writer's Digest. 9933
Alliance Road, Cincinnati, OH 45242.

Before you purchase any of these books, it might
be a good idea to check a library or bookstore to determine if they meet your individual needs.

One of the secrets of good writing is to avoid repeating words in the same sentence or paragraph. A
thesaurus, a book of synonyms and antonyms, will
help you find other words with the same meanings.
However, in some cases, word repetition is a genuine
aid to achieving effectiveness in speaking and writing.

TAPE RECORDER

A tape recorder allows a public relations practitioner to record a meeting or interview. However, it
also has some drawbacks. A person with such electronic equipment has a tendency to record every last word,
including all the small talk and jokes. When he wishes
to play back the tape, he must sit through the entire
meeting again to obtain the desired information. Often
it is more efficient to make notes of the highlights of a
meeting or interview with pencil and pad.

SHOPPING IT OUT

You are caught on the horns of a dilemma. You feel
you need a public relations campaign to project a favorable image to the public about your business. You
have neither the time to spare nor great PR expertise.
And you also realize that none of your employees possess the necessary skills to conduct a successful PR
operation. Without a doubt, it is time to consider
hiring a professional PR practitioner from outside
your firm. But, how do you go about it? You know little
about public relations. You don't know anything about
the PR agencies in your region. Even if you did, you
wouldn't know how to proceed.

Ron Palmquist of Cape Elizabeth, former president of the Maine Public Relations Council, points out

that limitations in time and PR skills are a good indication that an owner should consider an external agency instead of an in-house PR operation. He notes that the Yellow Pages, other business people, professional societies, chambers of commerce, and the U.S. Small Business Administration are possible sources of information about public relations agencies.

David Ferguson, president of the Public Relations Society of America (PRSA), agrees with the experience criterion. "A firm might decide on an in-house operation if it has someone inside with a background or flair for public relations," he said.

In addition to PRSA, other professional PR societies include the International Association of Business Communicators and Women in Communications. Check your telephone book for local chapters of these professional organizations.

In the 1985 edition of *Effective Public Relations* by Cutlip, Center and Broom, Chester Burger, a New York consultant to the PR field, lists six reasons why organizations retain firms, even though some have internal departments:

1. Management has not previously conducted a formal public relations program and lacks experience in organizing one.
2. Headquarters may be located away from the communications and financial centers of the nation.
3. A wide range of up-to-date contacts are maintained by an agency.
4. An outside agency can provide services of experienced executives who would be unwilling to move to other cities or whose salaries could not be afforded by a single firm.
5. An organization with its own public relations department may be in need of highly specialized services that it cannot afford on a permanent basis.

6. Crucial matters of overall outside policy dictate a need for the independent judgment of an outsider.

Agencies regard their variety of talents and skills as the greatest advantage over an internal operation. They also consider their objectivity as a relatively free agent a favorable factor in comparison with politics within a company. Other advantages cited by professional PR agencies are their range of previous experience, the geographical scope of their operations, the ability to reinforce and upgrade a client's internal staff, and their flexibility. They also emphasize their ready access to printing shops, copy editors and writers, placement specialists, artists or models, talk-show experts, and lawyers. Another major advantage is the reputation of an outside agency. External practitioners often can introduce ideas that internal staffers have failed to implement.

Public relations counseling has its obstacles. The professional often encounters opposition from insiders to new ideas, new approaches, and new looks. Resistance to change on the part of the old guard is a natural human characteristic and many practitioners regard it as their most serious handicap. Counselors also face questions of cost, resistance to outside advice, conflicts of personality or conviction, lack of understanding of public relations by clients, and the unavailability of clients when decisions are needed.

Measuring the quality of an outside public relations agency is, at best, a nebulous undertaking, especially to the owner of a new business whose exposure to the profession is limited to what he observes on television or in the movies. However, certain guidelines might help you to select the best firm for your company. In the area of competence and reputation, you might check samples of their work, experience with accounts similar to yours, length of time in business, size, scope of operation (local, regional, national or international), services and specialties that they offer, suppliers, types of accounts, and pattern of growth and financial stability. You might ponder the questions of cost, measurement of results, method of reporting progress and understanding of your objectives and needs.

The nature of the firm's clients also is an important consideration. You could examine lists of present and past clients, average length of client-firm relationships, average number during the past year, oldest clients, and those lost in the last 12 months. Another basis of selection is the qualification of the outside PR firm's staff. Turnover, former employees, backup, staff and percent of their time to be assigned to your account could be studied.

Jack O'Dwyer, editor of *Jack O'Dwyer's Newsletter* and *O'Dwyer's Directory of Public Relations Firms,* suggests another way for a client to shop for a PR agency. Contact reporters, editors, or news directors at local newspapers, magazines, radio, and television stations, and the trade press for your industry. Find out which PR firms are presently doing good work, who the reporters trust, who is in daily contact with the reporters, and who is considered an expert. It is a good idea to talk to more than one reporter in case one is partial to a particular PR firm.

Your own business associates also can give you a line on the better PR professionals. One firm is not necessarily better because it is larger. There are good PR firms in all sizes of agencies. Check each agency and pick the ones with special skills, location and size which fit your needs. If a firm is growing, that is an indication that it is doing good work. Agencies get more business through recommendations by current clients. The fact that an agency isn't growing could mean that these referrals are not forthcoming.

Select a few of these agencies from *O'Dwyer's Directory of Public Relations Firms* and examine their account lists. Look for clients in similar industries and determine if yours would fit in with the others. Compare account lists of the agencies and those of a few years ago to see if they retain at least some of their clients.

Public relations agencies should release complete lists of their clients. There is no good reason why they shouldn't. In fact, they could have no continuing clients or a poor record of retaining them. Or they could be hiding a conflict with your account. Professional PR practitioners should be able to submit up-to-date lists of their clients, contacts and telephone numbers.

The listing of an agency should contain real accounts, real people and real branch offices. If it includes clients from bygone days, minor projects, "staff members" who are actually freelancers or future employees on standby in case your account comes in, or "branches" that turn out to be affiliates over which the agency has little control, it might be well to consider another agency. The agency is misrepresenting itself and most likely handles its accounts in the same manner. Some PR firms give a false impression of their size by reporting a network of affiliates throughout the country ready to do their bidding. In no way does an affiliate even compare with the efficiency of a branch office.

THE PR SEARCH

Methods of finding a good PR firm vary from company to company. One invites four or five agencies to separate meetings, asks them about themselves and determines the extent of rapport between the company and agency. The company then selects two or three agencies with which it feels comfortable and asks them to submit written proposals for PR programs and ideas. The choice is made on the basis of the quality and originality of their ideas.

The PR director of another company looks for the agencies that get the important new accounts and do good work. He then calls in a few of them for a talk, checks their account lists, and takes written proposals.

One consultant to the PR field, who has helped many companies pick PR firms, cautions clients to ascertain that the agency really wants the business. He pointed out that some PR firms act as if they are doing you a favor by taking on your company. "If they act this way in the beginning, how will they act after six months or a year? Pick a firm that wants to work for you and will work hard to justify your confidence."

The consultant also advised prospective clients to inspect samples of the agency's work, look at the experience of the personnel who will be working with you, observe the length of time they hold clients, and judge whether or not the personality of the firm is compatible with your own. "Some clients prefer a super-agressive firm. Others like a more conservative approach. Which is right for you? Everything else being equal, the right match can make the difference between success and failure," he added.

A New York PR counselor advocates a visit to the offices of two or three finalist agencies to judge their size and strength before the client makes a decision. Empty offices, outdated clippings on the wall, and staff reading magazines are bad signs, he said. Good signs, according to the counselor, are busy typewriters, many incoming telephone calls, and modern copying machines, mailing, and collating equipment.

CLIENT MISCONCEPTIONS

Clients often hire an agency to alleviate PR problems that have existed for years, then expect the practitioner to solve them almost overnight. Public relations is basically an effort that produces long-term results, while advertising generally has a short-term effect.

Company representatives who engage outside agencies often don't know much about the PR profession. The people trying to sell the account often are not the ones who will be working on it. Consequently, the inexperienced people from the prospective client company are faced with the best salespeople from the agency. The company's decision often results in a bad match because it was based on superficial reasons.

On occasion, companies don't really need a PR firm because going outside won't solve their internal problems nor correct anti-communications attitudes in the company.

Some clients believe that the quality of a PR agency increases with its size. That is not necessarily true. The ability of the individuals within the agency is a more accurate criterion.

During agency briefings, clients have a tendency to withhold important information. This often results in later presentations that are not quite right.

Public relations companies sometimes don't get an opportunity to properly advise clients. They are encouraged to tell clients what they want to hear rather than what they need.

Clients have no idea of the cost of a good PR program. They want too much too soon for too little.

Companies frequently confuse advertising and public relations. Public relations often can be much more effective than advertising at a fraction of the cost.

Search committees set up by companies to find suitable PR agencies for their firms generally are too large. The quest often becomes party time in the big city for deserving company executives. A bad choice may be forthcoming if the committee sees too many agencies in too little time and makes its decision in the middle of a hangover.

PR FIRMS ON VIDEOTAPE

Operations of more than 20 major public relations firms have been videotaped to aid prospective clients in the search for agencies. Prepared by Public Relations Register of New York, the 10-minute videotapes and written presentations can be seen in confidence to avoid hurt feelings and follow-up calls by rejected or unqualified agencies. The clients may view PR firms in action without them knowing they are under scrutiny.

THE FINAL SELECTION PROCESS

At this point, you probably have a good idea about what makes a good PR firm and the type that best suits your company. But, before you make a final decision, you might want to ponder a few more thoughts.

Examine your own weaknesses and strengths in order to fully assess your needs. Are you strong in media relations but weak in writing skills? Do you have anyone on your staff who could do a company newsletter?

Make sure you are completely clear on the fee structure submitted by the firm you have in mind. The costs of retaining an outside firm to do your public relations will be covered later in this chapter.

Be wary of firms that promise too much. There is no way they can guarantee a story in the business section of *The New York Times* or even your local newspaper. There are too many factors involved.

Before signing a contract with the firm you have selected, make sure they are fully aware of your company's goals and what you expect of the firm. Develop a plan of action which includes both priorities and creative direction. Also, make sure the goals are realistic within the limitations of the budget and timetable.

If you have any ideas or suggestions for public relations, share them, by all means, with the agency you have selected. No one knows your business better than you.

Let your PR firm know your opinions about their programs and what they have to do to satisfy you.

Go into the specifics of your account. Determine who will be doing the work on a day-to-day basis. Insist that the senior member of the firm be involved in the implementation and follow-up phase of important projects.

Investigate the financial stability of the PR firm you have in mind. Check their Dun and Bradstreet credit rating, their most important vendors, and if they pay their bills on time. They should be financially stable enough to meet the needs of growth and expansion as well as your own account.

If they apply to your organization, determine the national and international capabilities of the firm. You may want public relations assistance in other sections of the United States or beyond.

The management of the firm should be involved in such professional organizations as the Public Relations Society of America, the International Association of Business Communicators, Women in Communications, or local, regional, and state groups. While membership in these organizations is not crucial, it does indicate leadership and concern for the profession. Peer recognition such as communications awards is also a sign of quality.

Specialization is another important factor to consider. Make sure the firm has what you are looking for, whether it be expertise in media relations, consumer and industrial marketing, employee relations, corporate and financial communications, graphics, community relations, or experience with nonprofit organizations.

The philosophy of the PR agency on public relations programming is another significant point. Do they thoroughly research their programs or do they play them by ear? While past experience is an important consideration, it should be coupled with adequate research. Public opinion surveys should be conducted to determine what people are saying about you and your competition. How do neighboring factories, stockholders, employees, and others perceive you?

Achieving and maintaining a successful relationship with the agency is a two-way responsibility. You and your PR agency should be in constant communication with each other. It means a commitment of time and money by both.

THE COST OF OUTSIDE PR

As an expanding business, you probably consider

the cost of engaging an outside public relations agency as the most important aspect of this chapter, if not the book. You are right. Then why, do you ask, is that question answered so late in the chapter? The reason is that you should have a proper foundation of information about the services and value of an outside agency before the question is addressed. Otherwise, the cost may turn you off immediately and you may not finish this book. Nobody works for nothing these days, including the professional PR counselor. And I've never heard of one starving to death.

As I've previously emphasized in this book, the reason for public relations is to fatten the bottom line. It's not something that happens overnight. Public relations is a long-range effort. Unlike advertising, it takes time to influence people's thinking. But, over the long haul, it is worth it. If you will bear with me and have a little confidence, I will show you how that bottom line will eventually grow to meet your expectations.

Now, let's get down to the nitty gritty. To begin with, fees of PR firms may range from a few hundred dollars a month to $5,000, $6,000 and more a month for the services of a major PR operation with multiple branch offices. Hill and Knowlton, Inc., of New York City, the largest agency, charges corporate clients a minimum of $5,000 a month, and association clients $6,000. This includes professional and support staff time multiplied by 3.2 times the person's hourly rate. Fees range from $55 to $175 an hour. Time after the minimum is reached is billed at the same rate. Expenses are billed at cost. Most of the clients must sign up for at least a year. If the client wishes to cancel the contract, he must give the firm 60 days notice. Most of the Hill and Knowlton clients are above these minimums. The agency maintains 19 domestic and 24 international branches and offers a full range of public relations work including a brochure for Bogle & Gates, a Seattle law firm with 133 attorneys.

Now, before you have some kind of seizure, let me emphasize that the New York-based Hill and

Knowlton is an international firm that I mentioned to provide a basis for comparison. Hiring an agency the size of Hill and Knowlton to project a favorable image for your expanding or newly-formed firm may be like trying to dispatch a gnat with a blast of 00 buckshot. If your target market is limited to the city or even the region, you certainly would not need a multi-national organization such as Hill and Knowlton. If you shop around, there is no reason why you couldn't find a competent practitioner at an hourly rate of $25 plus costs. He or she probably would not be able to exercise much influence on the minds of the general population of Timbuktu, but in your service area, the smaller PR operation would fully satisfy your needs.

Ron Palmquist, a professional PR counselor from Cape Elizabeth and a former president of the Maine Public Relations Council, charges his clients an hourly rate. "The first hour is free to give the client an idea of what it will cost and give me an idea of the client's PR needs," he explained. "For example, what is his marketing area and what is the best way to reach his market?"

As a further basis of comparison, I would like to explain the fee structures of some other PR agencies. Another large New York agency, Carl Byoir & Associates, Inc., has 10 domestic and four international branches. Both corporate and association clients pay a minimum of $5,000 a month, against which professional time is charged. The staff time is multiplied about three times the rate of hourly pay for overhead and profits. Byoir also has a unit called Business Organization, Inc., to handle smaller assignments. Their minimum is $4,000.

Both Hill and Knowlton and Byoir are subsidiaries of advertising agencies. Ruder Finn & Rotman, Inc., of New York City, the largest independent PR firm, does not have fixed monthly minimums in an effort to maintain flexibility. Basically, the firm charges for professional time. The agency also will adjust the charges to a set monthly bill if the work load can be readily predicted. Ruder Finn & Rotman maintains three branches.

Kanan, Corbin, Schupak & Aronow, a medium-sized agency, attempts to set a flat monthly fee that includes all services. Out-of-pocket expenses such as travel and production are billed separately. Under this system, the firm strives to accomplish the client's goals no matter how many hours or people involved in the account. After a time period, an adjustment will be sought if too much or too little time is being spent on the client. At Kanan, Corbin, Schupak & Aronow, effective product promotion programs normally cost from $3,000 to $5,000 with expenses running 20 to 25 percent more.

In a directory containing the names of 40 large, well-established public relations firms throughout the United States, hourly rates ranged from a low of $25 to a high of $175. And monthly retainers ranged from $1,000 to $10,000.

As you can see, there are wide variations in fees. Yet, PR firms may offer minimal services such as writing an occasional news release for as little as $100. The hourly fees range from $25 an hour for assistant account executives or other junior staffers to several hundred dollars for each hour put in by senior counselors and firm principals. Although the figures vary from region to region, four aspects are included in counseling fees and charges. These are cost of staff used on the project, executive time and supervision, overhead costs, and a reasonable profit for the work.

Four basic ways that a public relations agency may charge for continuing services are:

1. Monthly retainer or service fee.
2. Straight hourly charges.
3. Retainer and a monthly charge for actual staff time at an hourly rate or per diem basis.
4. A monthly fee plus increments for services performed beyond the retainer.

Public relations agencies have a wide range in

methods of charging for services because PR is still a new profession and involves a wide variety of possible functions for clients. By the same token, there is a wide variance in the rates that are charged. In general, the rates depend on the reputation and caliber of the firm, but do not necessarily reflect the quality of the service to be provided.

There are both chargeable and nonchargeable expenses in a PR agency. Those that can be charged to a client include meetings with clients to prepare material for the account, interviews, surveys and placement of materials, supervision of mailing and distribution of releases, photography assignments and other visual material prepared for the client, travel time to and from the client's office, and time spent during evenings and weekends with the client and his business.

Expenses which should not be charged to the client include maintaining liaison with the media, office and staff meetings and other group conferences related to PR business in general, solicitation of new business and the preparation of materials for potential clients, seminars, meetings, time spent on agency matters, and other professional activities. If a professional stays in a hotel during his own leisure time or participates in a purely social activity with a client, it would not be fair of him to bill for the expense.

You might keep in mind that it is more difficult for a PR agency to turn a profit working for a small business than with a large one. Smaller companies have little experience in the use of public relations services. They often make unreasonable demands and expect extraordinary results. Also, because of size, their activities have less news value or media interest than the larger companies.

For this reason, PR firms try to concentrate their efforts in areas where they can get demonstrable results. These include trade publications, weeklies, locally-produced Sunday supplements, and other regional media. Another possibility for the small business is a feature that might be appropriate for a local television "magazine" program.

Because of a small company's limited scope and appeal, the PR practitioner has to do a better selling job on such features to the print and television media. The PR professional also will work with the small business to develop programs that will generate publicity and foot traffic. A simple internal communications program like a newsletter will help company morale.

Small companies also have small PR budgets. The outside PR agency will help you make every penny count. It will advise you on how to use advertising economically, because you are going to need the effectiveness of a paid-for message. The PR professional will keep a watch on your pocketbook. Small budgets can't absorb things like printing overruns on expensive mass mailings.

PURE VALUE BILLING

Some public relations counselors are following the example of law, accounting, and management consulting firms in the evolution of a new method of charging clients called "pure value billing." Under this system, the client pays for the perceived value of the service provided instead of a set hourly rate or a retainer.

Jacob L. Engle, Jr., executive vice-president of Ketchum Public Relations, told more than 140 counselors at the 1984 annual spring conference of the Counselors Academy of the Public Relations Society of America that they should consider the new methods and build "flexibility" into their billing practices. "If you're tied into a rigid system such as billing by the hour only, you're going to leave an awful lot of money on the table," he said.

Engle noted that he once helped a client prevent a lengthy strike by counseling him for less than an hour. He also pointed out that PR people sometimes make placements on the "Today" show and in major media by working only for a brief time. Engle mentioned a willingness on the part of clients to pay for the "perceived value" of such achievements. When clients are faced with major matters related to their business, they are not concerned with the price, Engle continued. They want the "brains" and "know-how" of the agency at this point, rather than the routine back-office work, he said. As long as the goal is attained, Engle said, they almost don't seem to care about the cost.

The executive suggested that PR firms follow the lead of law firms by charging differently for the categories or work rather than by the hourly rate of the people involved in the various projects. Practitioners at the session stated that several PR firms specializing in mergers and acquisitions or in gaining access to top government officials in Washington already seem to be charging for "pure value."

COST-EFFECTIVENESS COMPARISONS

You are now at the stage of this chapter where you know what it costs to hire an outside public relations agency. And you know the equipment and personnel needed to run an in-house operation. Let's see if we can find some basis of comparison to help you make a decision on whether to go outside or delegate the PR chores to your staff or take them on yourself.

To begin with, if you or your staff have neither the time nor the skills needed to do your own PR, the decision may already have been made for you automatically. However, if you do have the time but not the skills, this book will help you acquire the necessary expertise.

As we have previously mentioned in this chapter, monthly retainers for established PR firms ranged from $1,000 to $10,000. For want of a better method of arriving at a monthly retainer for an outside agency to do the PR for your company, I am going to suggest an arbitrary figure of $3,000 a month or $36,000 a year. The $36,000 would cover just the time of the professional practitioner and his staff. There is no point in bringing the additional cost of printing, travel, advertising, and other expenses into the comparison because they would be present with both an in-house or outside PR operation.

Now, if you engaged an external organization to do your PR, we should assume they would do a first class job. If they didn't, you made a poor choice. In order to match the quality of the outside operation, you would, at the very least, need a public relations director and a secretary for an internal job. If you are personally doing the PR, you would have to deduct a proportionate amount of time from your company duties for that task.

Let's say that you can get a good PR director for an annual salary of $25,000. How much would we have to pay the PR secretary? How about $18,000? Adding up these figures, we come up with $36,000 plus costs for an outside agency and $43,000 plus costs for an inside operation.

In this particular case, the figures would seem to favor an outside agency. In your locality, it may cost you more or less than $36,000 a year for an outside PR agency and you may be able to pick up a good PR director and secretary for more or less than $43,000. You will have to fill in the blanks yourself.

There is one other factor of course. If you are a small company there is a good chance you have a very limited PR budget. With an in-house operation, you have more control over your public relations and you can fit the operation to your budget. You probably won't have enough public relations for your company but, as I have said before, public relations is like true love, friendship, and apple pie. You never have enough of it. So you have to be realistic and do what you can afford.

MONITORING THE OUTSIDE AGENCY

You have made a decision to engage an external agency to project a favorable image of your company.

But that doesn't mean that you can suddenly wash your hands of anything to do with public relations and go on to other company duties. As head of your business, you are ultimately responsible for your company PR and you should have control over it. That means you must constantly audit and monitor the performance of the external PR agency you have hired.

Ron Palmquist suggests that the client could keep his finger on the pulse of the PR operation by asking the professional practitioner for a monthly report. In fact, a business owner should demand as many status reports as he feels are necessary to maintain control. These could include conference reports after each major meeting to firmly fix deadlines, priorities, responsibilities, and budgets for major assignments.

Public relations is, at best, an inexact science. The practitioner deals with attitudes, striving to favorably impact attitudes of a variety of publics. There are many ways of measuring the performance of a PR firm, but some are so cumbersome and costly that they would take more time and money to complete than the PR effort itself.

One New York PR counselor maintains that for $5,000 or $6,000 a month, an agency should be able to produce four or five major placements a year. This would be in addition to the counseling, product, personnel, and other routine announcements. By major placements, also described as "home runs" of the profession, we mean stories in *The New York Times, The Boston Globe, The Wall Street Journal, Time* or *Newsweek,* or a spot on a nationwide television program. Stories in the major, general circulation media are the most efficient way to reach large audiences.

Although it is easier to get stories in trade journals because they are understaffed and badly in need of material, they don't have the readership of other media. The company may be an advertiser in the magazine and can easily get editorial coverage through pressure. The company also may be so important in the field that trade journals have to print everything it says.

Public relations firms are inclined to relax their efforts for a while after a major placement for a company. There is a tendency for them to say, "That should hold them for a while." It is up to you, as head of the business, to continue pressure on your PR agency. Give them information as often as you can.

In addition to monthly reports on what has happened and what has been proposed, and monthly meetings with the agency, they should offer a yearly program, and a six-month briefing with a forecast on the next six months. At least one or two creative ideas should be included in the monthly reports.

Although it is difficult to measure the results of public relations, it is possible if done properly. The measurement helps to establish cost-effective activities. The first step is to make sure that we have done our homework. Before public relations can be programmed intelligently, we need to conduct adequate research to understand the area. We want to know who is in the area, what they think of our company, and what effect previous communications from our firm have had on the area. Benchmark surveys provide a datum level that gives us a basis of comparison or reference point to help measure the results of new programs. The survey frequently takes the form of a communications audit, which can be conducted by mail, telephone, through personal interviews or a combination of all these methods.

Another way to measure the performance of a public relations firm, especially with heavy publicity programs, is to measure the amount of printed space and air time on television and radio generated by the agency through the publicity program. The degree to which the exposure has improved both in quantity and quality over previous efforts offers a definite measurement of current public relations effectiveness.

The lineage and air time surveys also can help you compare the effectiveness of your publicity dollars with advertising costs. As you make your comparison, keep in mind one important point. The credibility level is higher in publicity programs than in paid advertising. The news or feature editors, in effect, put a stamp of approval on your company and product or service by favorable editorial exposure through their respective communications media. This believability component can only be enhanced through publicity techniques.

American Telephone & Telegraph Co. conducted a public relations measurement program for years through standardized measurement of administrative costs, attitude perceptions, and the testing of interest, readability and readership comprehension of employee publications.

"But," you say, "it is ridiculous to compare my company with AT&T. They have the resources to run an extensive survey like this. I don't." You are wrong. Even with a small operation, you could measure the results of your PR program, though to a lesser degree. Why couldn't your secretary make a few telephone calls? Or why couldn't you talk to a few people on the street? And, as far as measuring publicity is concerned, I bet your spouse would be thrilled to help the company by keeping track of its exposure in the print media or on air time.

MONITORING YOUR PR FIRM

In evaluating the performance of the agency that handles your company's public relations, you should concentrate on certain areas. The agency should follow a systematic method in the analysis of client needs and planning programs. The method should be in written form and be understood by all members of your firm. The agency should make a distinct effort to understand your business and industry, seeking information from you and other sources on your product, service, customers, marketing, distribution, and positioning. Their proposals should show an understanding of the business problem as well as the publicity problem. Research should be used effectively to identify the problem, target audience and media, understand attitudes, evaluate obstacles and opportunities, and develop positions. The programs should be planned around clearly defined positions and themes. The agency should measure results by the effect on target audiences as well as in terms of media coverage.

In the implementation of the programs, you should determine if the topics are tailored for the target audience and if they support the program objectives. Press materials should be written in good style and grammar without typographical errors. Support materials such as photos and captions should be consistent in style and presentation.

Materials sent to the media should be selectively targeted so they will reach your potential clients or customers. The agency should maintain good up-to-date media lists. The staff should have contact with media representatives on an informal basis. When they mail out material, the agency should check its disposition by the media. Programs should be conducted on schedule and materials and placement activities should be coordinated to support program and business objectives.

The agency you have hired to do your public relations should keep its own house in order. The PR firm should do a good job of managing its own business, critical resources, and services for clients. And the agency should secure the best resources to meet the needs of your company, even if it has to go outside its own staff. Senior management should be involved with your account, attending meetings with you in order to know what is transpiring at the account level.

Your PR agency should be realistic about its own limitations, being careful not to make promises it cannot keep. The chemistry should be good between members of your company and the PR firm. The PR professionals should be enthusiastic about your account and enjoy working with you. By the same token, you should have confidence in them.

You should examine the agency's turnover rate with clients and their own employees. Other factors

which should be studied are the PR firm's effective
use of time, the clarity and accuracy of their bills, adherence to budget, response to client needs, and pro-
vision of written plans and accountable objectives.

CHAPTER

4

4

The Public
Relations Product

Now it is time for you to roll up your sleeves and get to work. As head of your company, you have the information you need to make a decision on whether to do the public relations yourself or hire an outside agency.

If your decision favored an in-house operation, you know how to select the best person to head your public relations effort. He or she may not be another Adolphus Busch, Joyce Hall, Lane Bryant or Soichiro Honda, but will be the best person you could find for the job.

If you decided that the company public relations needs your personal touch, you have made a commitment to reserve enough time for this important chore. And, if you are short on experience but tall in enthusiasm, Chapter 4 was written especially for you. It will give you the tools you need to conduct a quality public relations program for your company.

An expanding business is like one of the Super Cub motorcycles manufactured by Soichiro Honda. It takes many tools to design and build the two-wheeled vehicle, maintain it in top shape, and repair it when it breaks down. Each tool has a specific purpose and the right size must be used on the right part.

As head of your business, you also must use the right public relations tools for the right job. For the long-range PR effect, you may want to use news releases and photos of your new plant and its operation, an open house, a story in the trade journal, or a brochure explaining your product or service.

A quick promotion may call for a paid advertisement in the newspaper. Keeping your business running on an even keel may require your services as a speaker at Rotary Club or Chamber of Commerce meetings, annual reports to your stockholders, and a series of news releases on new personnel, promotions, and service anniversaries.

And, God forbid, if you should have big problems such as the Tylenol tragedy or needles in Girl Scout cookies, you may try to repair the damage by purchasing television time to emphasize the security measures you have taken.

ATTRACTING THE MEDIA

There is one sure method of bringing the media to your place of business on the run. Just make them aware of a major news story about to break. Unfortunately, a major news story often does not have the desired public relations value.

Your mission, of course, is to attract the media to something that will cast you, your company and your product or service in a favorable light. Sometimes it is as simple as picking up a telephone and calling the media. If time permits, the city editor or news director also would appreciate a note they could set aside to study later in the day when they weren't so busy. The message containing information about a possible story could be similar in format to the type of memo you might send to a member of your company staff.

In both cases, you should prepare a news release to hand to the media representative. Don't bother to call them about a routine story. Just give them a news release.

There are ways of attracting the media to some degree. However, the question of whether or not they make an appearance will hinge on several factors including the size and scope of your company, its impact on the community, the number of persons it hires, the reader interest, the news value of the potential story, the availability of a reporter and a photographer, and the number of other important stories occurring on that same day.

A groundbreaking ceremony to mark the beginning of the construction of a new plant to build flangemeters for the Colonial Gidget Co. may do the trick. But let's come up with some fresh ideas. Bury the timeworn routine of having the company president or mayor remove the first bit of earth with a gold-plated shovel. Since the flangemeters are going to be used in the Space Shuttle, maybe you could find an astronaut to preside over the ceremony.

You might even wait until the plant opens to have a big ceremony. Then you could combine the ceremony with an open house, tours of the plant, and demonstrations and exhibits of how flangemeters are manufactured from the raw stock to the finished product. It would give you an opportunity to show the meticulous inspection of each instrument before it leaves the plant.

Other special events such as anniversaries, annual meetings, forums, seminars, award programs, and competitions also might draw the media to your place of business. But, as I have said before, use your imagination and creativity to develop something different.

THE NEWS RELEASE

Of the many tools at the disposal of the public relations person, probably the most basic is the news release. Some PR practitioners prefer to call them press releases. I am partial to "news release" because I define press as a name for the print media only. "News" covers all the media — press, radio and TV.

But before we get into the intricacies of writing news releases, let me emphasize one point: *First try to get the media to do the story themselves.* They are the professionals in their field. Their business is covering the news. Yours is manufacturing or servicing gidgets. And if you are better than they are at covering the news, you're in the wrong business.

Perhaps you have tried to interest the media in sending members of their staffs to cover what you believed to be a good news story. They have declined for what could have been a number of reasons. Probably the biggest reason was that the story did not have sufficient news value to staff it. Or there could have been a manpower problem. Members of the news staff might already have been occupied in covering another story. Often, however, an editor may say he would be more interested in the story if you can send some information about it. That is your cue for a news release. That is also your first lesson in media relations, which will be covered in depth later in this chapter.

Even if the media agree to send a reporter, you should prepare a news release as a handout. The reporter will appreciate the basic information; it saves time and provides a starting point for the story. Be prepared to answer many more questions about your story. The media may even ask for answers that are already in your news release. Don't worry about it. They just want the answers in your own words so they can insert direct quotes into the story. It adds color and brings the reader into the action. In other words, it gives the reader the feeling that he is listening to you directly as head of the company.

WRITING THE NEWS RELEASE

If you already have had a course in basic journalism in high school or college or a public relations workshop or seminar, this may not be new to you. However, please bear with me because we can all stand a review on the fundamentals of newswriting.

In writing a news release, we ask six basic questions:

1. *Who?*
2. *What?*
3. *When?*
4. *Where?*
5. *Why?*
6. *How?*

The six questions, commonly called "the five *W*s and the *H*," will give you enough information to write the first paragraph or "lead" of a story.

If you have ever been in the newsroom of a newspaper, you probably have seen reporters sitting in front of typewriters or VDT's (video display terminals) with puzzled looks on their faces. Most likely, they were in the process of writing leads. The lead is the most important part of a story and much care should be taken in writing it. In fact, the lead should be able to stand alone as a complete story. Many veteran journalists say that when they get the lead written, the rest of the story writes itself. The lead of a story does not have to be crammed into a single sentence. It should continue until the five *W*s and the *H* are answered. Generally, every story does have four *W*s. They can either be apparent or understood. Not every story has a why or a how, but if they do, they should be answered. Now, let's try a sample lead and see if we can find the five *W*s and the *H*:

ANYTOWN-The Colonial Gidget Co. (Who?), a manufacturer of precision instruments, will conduct an open house (What?) Saturday (When?) to show (Why?) its new Main Street plant (Where?).

The program, open to the public, will begin at 9 a.m. with guided tours and demonstrations (How?). Company President John E. Smith will be on hand to answer questions.

Do you get the idea? As you conduct your interview or research to get information for your story, you can ask these six questions. I am going to make a few more points before we practice writing leads. In journalism, the writing should be crisp and concise. Use as few words as possible to tell your story fully. The first sentence should average about 30 words. Write your leads and then edit them by trying to tell the same story in fewer words. We call this tightening up the copy. Another rule is to write objectively rather than subjectively. Don't use first person pronouns such as "I" or "we" except within a direct quotation.

Now, I'm going to suggest a few exercises to give you some practice in writing leads. Take the following information in each example and write a lead:

1. The Federal Deposit Insurance Corp. has proposed a policy change. The proposal was made yesterday. The change would make it easier for small banks to merge. The change would make it more difficult for large banks to merge. The proposal was made at an FDIC board meeting. The meeting was held in Washington. The proposal calls for the addition of two components to the agency's evaluation of merger applications. The competition from all types of financial services companies in a particular market would be taken into account. The FDIC would evaluate the "potential" competitive effect of a big bank into a new market.

2. Robert F. Daniell will become chief executive officer of United Technologies Corp. United Technologies is based in Hartford, Conn. Daniell is president and chief operating officer of United Technologies. The appointment will become effective January 1. Daniell will succeed Harry J.

Gray. Gray has been leader of United Technologies for a long time. Gray will remain chairman.

3. Eight-week course. The subject of the course is defensive driving. The course will be sponsored by the Maine Safety Council. The course will be held on Monday, July 29. The course will run from 8 a.m. to 5 p.m. Holiday Inn West, Exit 8, will be the location of the course.

This information was taken from leads of actual stories which appeared in newspapers. The first two were in *The Wall Street Journal* and the third was in *The Maine Sunday Telegram* of Portland, Maine. Compare your leads with theirs:

1. WASHINGTON-The Federal Deposit Insurance Corp. proposed changing its policy to make bank mergers easier among small banks and more difficult for large ones.

Under the proposal made at the FDIC's board meeting yesterday, two components would be added to the agency's evaluation of merger applications: The FDIC would take into account the competition from all types of financial services companies in a particular market, and it would evaluate the "potential" competitive effect of the entry of a big bank into a new market.

2. HARTFORD, Conn.-United Technologies Corp. said Robert F. Daniell, president and chief operating officer, will become chief executive officer Jan. 1, succeeding the company's long-time leader Harry J. Gray, who will remain chairman.

3. The Maine Safety Council will hold an eight-hour defensive driving course Monday, July 29, from 8 a.m. to 5 p.m. at Holiday Inn West, Exit 8, Portland.

Don't be concerned if your leads did not match *The Wall Street Journal* and *The Maine Sunday Telegram* leads word for word. There are probably several correct ways of writing a lead with the same information. Now take your own local newspaper and observe the leads in the stories. The five *W*s and the *H* may not be as clearly defined as those in the first two examples I gave you.

But, if you read on in the stories, you will find most of them are there or are understood.

To get the meaning of "understood" clear in your mind, let me give you an example. The United Technologies story says that Daniell will become chief executive officer. In answer to the question of "how?" the story implies the understanding that Daniell was elected to the post by the board of directors.

Now that we know how to write a lead, let's see what we can do with the rest of the story. Most of your news releases will be written in what is called the inverted pyramid style of newswriting. Think of an upside down pyramid. In this style, we begin with the lead and write the rest of the story in descending order of importance. We start with the most important part of the story and end with the least important.

There are some very good reasons for this style of newswriting. First, an editor who is making up a newspaper page is usually working against a deadline and probably has a limited amount of space. Your story may be longer than the available space. Thus, your story can be shortened quickly by deleting the last paragraph. If the story still is too long, the editor can delete the next paragraph from the bottom and so on. In fact, he can eliminate all but the lead and still have a complete story. It just won't give as much detail.

Second, the inverted pyramid style of newswriting accommodates the reader. Most people don't have enough time or interest to read the whole newspaper and each story in its entirely. Generally, they will skim through the newspaper reading the headline and lead in each story. The lead will give them the gist of the story. If the story interests them, they will read the rest of it.

The more news releases you write the quicker you will be able to recognize the importance of the various points in the story. For an example, let's go back to our story about the opening of the new plant of the Colonial Gidget Co. You probably would follow up the lead with the quotes from company President John Smith and the mayor, report the number of people who will be employed there, how the plant will affect the town tax base, its the physical dimensions, something about its operations, maybe identify the plant manager, and give some background on the company and the president. You might end up with refreshments being served to the public. Quite often, the refreshments fall victims of the copy editor's pencil or cursor.

Another style of writing is the rectangular style. This style is more commonly called a feature story or feature writing. The writer starts with a literary type of lead which does not sum up the story in the manner of the lead of the inverted pyramid. The story continues with information of equal importance, more or less. If you have had no previous experience in creative writing, I suggest that you make a strong attempt to interest the media in doing features themselves. Again, we will cover this subject in a discussion of media relations later in this chapter.

There is still a third style of writing that journalists call the pyramid, "bright" or "sidebar." I am sure you have listened to thousands of jokes where the punch line or most important part is at the very end. That is exactly the form of a bright. It is just a joke in writing, with the most important part at the end of the story to form a pyramid. Brights often are set in a bold type on page 1 and rarely run more than a half dozen paragraphs in length.

There are several other variations in newspaper writing that you, in your public relations efforts, would not have to master. They include the news feature where a feature story also has a high news value, an analysis or interpretive piece usually written by an editor or reporter who specializes in that particular subject (a business writer in your case), an editorial where the media cite their opinions, a column, and a first-person story written by the individual about a dramatic, unusual, or dangerous experience. Although you probably would not be writing these types of stories personally, it is well worth the effort to persuade the media to write an editorial, column, analysis, or news feature which would cast your company in a favorable light.

At this point, I would like to emphasize that you or the person in your company who does the public relations should have a good command of the English language and the fundamentals of grammar before attempting a news release. An English course is beyond the scope of this book. Even professional journalists have mastered these fundamentals long before they enter journalism school.

The purpose of this chapter is to introduce you to some of the skills you will need to write a news release in a professional journalistic style. The only way to learn these skills is to write, write and write until the words come out of your ears. If you or the PR person in your company do not possess these skills, I would strongly suggest that you look into the possibility of engaging an external practitioner. It would do more harm than good to distribute poorly written news releases to the media.

Now that we have some idea about how a news release should be written, let's get down to the finer points. If you plan to send out many news releases, you should probably have printed letterheads containing the name and address of your company, branches, brand name, trademark or logo, the name and telephone number of a person who can be called for further information (yourself or PR person), and the words, "News Release." If you do not have a printed letterhead, just type at the left top of the first page the words, "For further information call:" followed by your name, address and telephone number.

Above all, never, never send a handwritten release to the media. Most newspapers receive more news releases than they can use and do not have enough personnel or time to unscramble and decipher someone else's handwriting. A handwritten release will swiftly find its way into the round file.

Start your story about two inches below the heading to give the editor space to designate the style of headline for your release. *Don't* try to write a headline yourself because you have no way of knowing the number of columns or style of headline which will fit the space and be appropriate to the story. You might "slug" the story with something like "Gidget open house" at the upper left hand corner of each page so the copy can be readily identified.

Never use onionskin or very thin paper for your release. All copy should be double-spaced with margins of at least one inch to give the copy desk room to make corrections or changes. Don't write on both sides of the paper. This creates problems for the editor. And don't break a paragraph between pages. Stories often are sent to the composing room one page or a "take" at a time and splitting up a paragraph increases the possibility of typographical errors.

ATTRIBUTION

If you can see, hear, feel, or taste it, or if it is an established fact, you don't need attribution. For everything else, you must attribute all information in your news release to a source. That is one of the rules of journalism. In your case, you would be the source because of your position as head of your company. Even if you have delegated the PR duties to another person in your company, you should be the spokesman.

When you mention a person's name for the first time in a news release, give first name, middle initial, last name, and identify the individual. And don't use nicknames unless they are enclosed within quotation marks after the first name. Nicknames are allowed only on the sports page of a newspaper. When you refer to the person a second time in a news release, you may use Mr. Smith, Smith, Mrs. Smith, Miss Smith, or Ms. Smith. As a result of the women's movement, it has also become acceptable in some newspapers to use just a woman's last name in a second reference. You should check the style of the newspaper to which you are sending the release. If your release is going to many newspapers, I would use the more conservative style of preceding a woman's last name with Miss, Mrs., or Ms.

Unfortunately, all newspapers in the United States do not adhere to the professional standards of *The Wall Street Journal* or *The New York Times.* I'm sure you have seen many newspapers which use nicknames in the general news section, ignore middle initials, and fail to identify a person properly. However, if your news releases reflect the highest standards of journalism, it will be a credit to both you and your company. Remember, the public judges you and your company by the quality of your work and presentation. A sloppy news release may indicate that you employ the same standards in your product or service.

RELEASE DATES

Some public relations people like to use release dates on their news releases. Beginning at the upper left hand margin, they type in full capital letters the words, "FOR IMMEDIATE RELEASE" or "RELEASE AT WILL" if the story is to be used as soon as it arrives. If the story is to be used on a specific date, they type something like "RELEASE ON MONDAY, JULY 29." I never like to use release dates at all. On very rare occasions, I have used release dates if a story about a lecture or other event was given to the media before it took place.

Probably my reluctance to use release dates stems from my experience as a newspaper reporter and editor in a highly competitive area covered by five daily and two weekly newspapers. Public relations people sent releases to all seven newspapers with release dates on the publication day of the weeklies. The idea, of course, was to release the stories to all the newspapers at the same time. Although they had good intentions, the point is that the dailies sometimes were asked to sit on a good, timely news story for as long as four or five days to wait for publication of the weeklies. I believe that a release date is an insult to the intelligence of the editor and an obvious attempt to manage the news. It is the prerogative of the media to use a story when they wish to do so.

The release date should be apparent by the content of the story. If it is a good story, it should be used immediately. If the story is of a routine nature, it should be held until time and space permits its publication.

Weekly newspapers have an advantage over dailies because they have the time to research continuing stories in depth, run more feature material, and use stories of a more personal nature. By the same token, dailies should use spot news, major stories, and other timely events in the next issue after they happen.

POLISHING THE RELEASE

As we have already stated, journalistic writing should be crisp and concise. Do not express your personal opinion in a news story. A newspaper bares its conscience on the editorial page or in a column. As much as possible, avoid adjectives, adverbs, passive verbs, and other words or sentence structures that might express opinion or increase the length of your release. Give the most facts in the fewest words. Short sentences containing a single thought are the essence of good journalistic writing.

Paragraphs should range from four to seven typewritten lines. However, that is not a hard and fast rule, only a guide. Generally, a lengthy paragraph should be followed by a short paragraph. Unless you are writing a major news story, there is little justification for a release of more than two pages. By a major news story, I mean something like the opening of a new plant, a merger with another firm, or a diversification which will create 200 new jobs in the area.

At the bottom of each page, you should type the word, "more," enclosed in parenthesis. This indicates to the editor that there are more pages to come. After the first page, you might number each page, slug it, and date it in the upper left hand corner as shown in Figures 4-1 and 4-2. At the end of the story, type the number 30 enclosed in hyphens, "–30 –." Another way to indicate the end of the story is to use the symbol: "#." These symbols show the editor that the story is concluded.

Figure 4-1: Sample Format for a News Release

COLONIAL GIDGET CO.
Anytown, Pa.

NEWS RELEASE

For further information call:
John E. Smith
President
(412) 978-2265
July 31, 1985

ANYTOWN-Harvey J. Brown, quality control manager of the Colonial Gidget Co. for 14 years, has been promoted to the new position of vice president of operations.

Company President John E. Smith, who announced the appointment, said, "The new position was created to take full advantage of Brown's many years of experience in the field of precision instruments." The appointment is effective immediately.

"In addition to overseeing the operations section of the plant, Brown will be responsible for setting up a new training program for quality control inspectors," Smith said. "Our new government contracts to provide instruments for the Space Shuttle have indicated a need for more quality control."

(more)

Figure 4-2: Sample Format for Page 2 of a News Release

Page 2
Colonial Gidget Promotion
July 31, 1985

Among other instruments, Colonial manufactures precision flangemeters and toggleswitches for the Shuttle's solar battery system.

Before joining Colonial Gidget, Brown was a member of the administrative staff of International Wombat Corp. He also was assistant professor of mechanical engineering at the University of Rhode Island. The new vice president came to Colonial Gidget in 1960 as a quality control inspector and rose through the ranks to his present position.

Brown holds both Master of Science and Bachelor of Science degrees from the Massachusetts Institute of Technology. His professional affiliations include the past presidency of the Pennsylvania Society of Mechanical Engineers and a directorship in the American Society of Mechanical Engineers. He also is a charter member of the Pennsylvania Gidgeteers.

Brown and his wife, the former Mary J. Hill of Philadelphia, are residents of 34 Main St. here. They have two children, Keith and Joan. Active in community affairs, Brown is president of the Anytown Kiwanis Club.

-30-

THE PRESS CONFERENCE

Have you ever given a party and nobody came? It's embarrassing to say the least. For that reason, be wary about setting up press conferences. In fact, if a news release or a telephone call will serve the same purpose, forget about the press conference. A reporter may have a half dozen major stories to write in the course of his day's work. He can handle a news release in a few minutes while a press conference may consume a couple of hours.

However, there are special situations when a press conference may be useful. If a major announcement is to be made and it is difficult to cover in a release, you might consider such an event. When a subject is so important that reporters should be given an opportunity to ask questions, you might schedule one. Another reason for a press conference is to give reporters an opportunity to meet, photograph, and question an important dignitary.

A press kit containing news releases, data sheets, photos, and other information should be available. If time permits, you can send invitations to city editors for newspapers and news directors for radio and TV. Otherwise, a telephone call will do. They will assign personnel if they wish to cover the event. Schedule the conference for midmorning to accommodate the evening newspapers or early afternoon for the morning newspapers. Your decision probably will hinge on the deadlines of the majority of the newspapers in your coverage area. Anything after 2 p.m. generally is difficult for the electronic media to process in time for the 6 o'clock news.

Schedule the conference at a centrally located site where it is easily accessible for media representatives. The room should have a lectern or other similar equipment. Provide sufficient seating for each media person and a few seats for uninvited media representatives. Limit access to the news media and company officials. Start the conference on time, conduct it in a professional manner, and give the media plenty of time to ask questions.

Go easy on the refreshments. Coffee and doughnuts are sufficient. Don't serve alcohol — media representatives are in the middle of their working day and the last thing they need is a mind full of cobwebs when they sit down to write stories.

THE TV NEWS EVENT

While the press conference should be used sparingly, the TV news event may be a more productive tool for your company's public relations effort. There is no reason why such an event can't be shared by newspapers and radio as well as TV. However, if newspaper reporters fail to attend the event, its success still will be assured by the appearance of TV personnel.

When you schedule the TV event, make sure the time is satisfactory for all TV stations in the area. There is nothing wrong in calling TV news directors to determine the best time for the event. Television stations don't have as much flexibility in scheduling as newspapers because they have crews and equipment to organize as well as reporters.

As a public relations person for one organization, I was able to arrange TV coverage on several occasions. I knew that the television crews would be in the area every Wednesday afternoon for the governor's news conference. So I scheduled events at that time and caught them on the return trip. We got the TV coverage and the TV stations were able to kill two birds with one stone.

When the TV crews arrive on the scene, make sure they have a visual target at which to aim their cameras. If you are announcing the construction of a new wing to the plant, prepare a model of the finished building. If you unveil a new product that is expected to revolutionize the industry, then, by all means, give them an opportunity to get some footage of that product. Costumes, works of art, demonstrations of manufacturing techniques, exhibits of how the flangemeter is used in the Space Shuttle, and other photogenic devices also are good visual targets for TV.

A press kit containing a news release on the story, data sheets, biographies of participating dignitaries, and other relevant material should be available to the TV crew as well as for newspaper and radio personnel.

Sometimes TV stations will use *key slides* of a company president or other important members of your firm to appear behind the newscaster as he gives his report. Check with the TV news director for the proper format.

DISSEMINATION OF NEWS

Where should you send your news releases? It seems we are back to the target market again. Remember the market grid? If your firm, the Imperial Machine Co., makes precision devices for fire engine pumpers, you may want to send your releases to major media and trade journals throughout the country. But, as the owner of McDonald's, you may choose only regional coverage to avoid duplication with franchisees of the same fast-food chain in other sections of the state. And, of course, Pete's Delicatessen would do well to limit its public relations to the local media.

If there are several newspapers, radio and television stations in your region, you should make an effort to be fair to all of them. You should give one good story to the morning papers first. The next time you have a good story it should go to the evening papers first. You can promise the weekly newspaper an exclusive depth story. See if the radio station might schedule you or a representative of your company for a talk show. And stage some kind of media event for the television station.

It's not easy. Trying to be fair to everyone takes a bit of juggling. But it will pay off in good media relations. And it will challenge your expertise in public relations.

Don't forget to put radio and television stations on the mailing list for your news releases. They won't use as many of them as the newspapers and when they do they may only use a sentence or two because of time limitations, but it is worth it.

If there is enough news value in the story, you may get a call from the news director of the radio station. He can tape by telephone your voice reading a paragraph or two from the story to broadcast over the air.

The story also might appeal to the TV news director. What could be better public relations than a telecast from your place of business?

You can find addresses of the media and trade journals in the reference books mentioned in Chapter 3. If you have many on your mailing list, it may be easier to place them in a computer. The computer printer will produce sheets of addressed labels to be transferred to envelopes. Postage meters that can be filled regularly at the Post Office also are helpful for large mailing lists.

WHAT IS NEWS?

This question seems to mystify a great many people. Perhaps they have good reason to be unsure about that hazy, gray line which often separates a good news story and a block of pure information.

There are a few guidelines to help us recognize that nebulous thing called "news." Most veteran reporters can immediately tell a story from a non-story. It hits you in the gut. It's not news when a woman's son uses drugs. It is news when she turns him in.

During my years as a general news reporter, one example stands out in my mind. Drug arrests were common occurrences in the turbulent '60s, and they still are for that matter. However, I can remember one case where a distraught mother discovered her son was abusing drugs. She turned her own son in to the police. You can imagine the mother's soul searching before she made that move. I am sure the son is a better man today as a result of her action. It also was a good human interest story and made page 1 instead of being buried in the inside pages like many minor drug arrests.

Although it wasn't a great story, the example serves to illustrate that one aspect of the case made the difference between a routine arrest and a good human interest yarn. That fact could easily have been overlooked on the police blotter.

Lest you get the impression that the boy and his mother were exploited by the newspaper just for the sake of a story, I would like to add that their names were not used in the write-up.

Some guidelines for recognizing a good news story are *timeliness, general interest, human interest,* and *unusualness.*

In order to be timely, a story should appear in print as soon as possible after it happens. If it is a daily newspaper, the story should be in the paper within 24 hours. For a weekly, the write-up should be in the next edition.

"Impossible," you say? "There is no way for me to get a company story in the paper within 24 hours." You are right. However, there are ways of writing your release so the time element will be up to date. The plans for the new Colonial Gidget Co. plant may have been received from the architect a week ago. But you can write that President Smith released or announced them "today."

You will notice that a daily newspaper will write stories so they seem to be as timely as possible. Something that happened yesterday morning will be "yesterday" in the evening paper and today's morning event will be "today." As a general rule, I would advise you to get your stories to the paper as soon as you can and write them in such a manner that they appear to be as timely as possible.

A news item that has wide general interest has a better chance of being used than one which would appeal only to a special interest group. When you write your story, stress the aspect that has the greatest interest for the largest number of people.

The human interest is an important consideration in judging the news value of a story. A good method of determining human interest is to place yourself in the position of the subject of a story and try to identify yourself with him. Would you do the same thing he did if confronted with the same situation?

Anything that is unusual or bizarre is certain to make a good story. For example, people know that John E. Smith is president of Colonial Gidget Co., but how many know that he plays Santa Claus at the local department store during Christmas time? Do they know that Colonial Gidget Co. hires blind persons to inspect flangemeters for the Space Shuttle? And do they know that the blind are better inspectors than the sighted because of their highly developed sense of touch? Go, Mr. President! Use your imagination. I bet you've got stories like that in your own company. They make great public relations and the media can't get enough of them.

Every story originating from your company doesn't fall into the page 1 category, of course. Most never attain that status. However, a constant flow of releases will keep a favorable image of your firm in the minds of the public. The acceptance by the media of some more or less routine stories will depend on the size of your company and its impact on the community. You might consider development of the following story ideas:

1. Promotions, appointments, and transfers.
2. Retirement of old employees.
3. Building activities.
4. Major equipment installations.
5. New products.
6. Annual statements.
7. Dividends declared.
8. Expansion programs.
9. Unusual orders.
10. Election of new directors or executives.
11. Meetings of the board.

12. Changes in work hours.
13. Safety records.
14. Unusual hobbies, pastimes, or avocations by company personnel.
15. Bonuses or Christmas gifts.
16. Pay raises.
17. Awards or recognition of the company.
18. New company processes, inventions, or experiments.
19. Company picnics, parties, dinners, banquets, or meetings.
20. Unusual production records.
21. Unusual shipments.
22. Addition of extra crews or night shifts.
23. Profit-sharing plans.
24. Training programs.
25. Company-sponsored sports, musical groups and clubs.
26. New labor contracts.
27. Company participation in charity or community activities.
28. Visits to your plant by celebrities.
29. Sales meetings and conventions.
30. New buying policies.
31. Major remodeling or improvement projects.
32. Activities of elderly employees.

This should give you some ammunition for your PR campaign. Actually, there is no end to story ideas. They go on and on. I'm sure you could come up with a few more ideas from your own company. The only limitations are time, personnel and money to implement them.

MEDIA RELATIONS

First of all, there are no deep, dark secrets or magic formulas for inducing the media to do nice stories about your company. Contrary to the beliefs of those who received their training in media relations from the movies or television, you don't whisper sweet nothings into the ears of reporters of the opposite sex, wine and dine them, let them beat you at golf, or offer them money to get favorable coverage.

If there is any system at all, it is the simple practice of common sense which will determine your progress toward that goal of obtaining good press. However, there is one fact which stands out above all others: *If your story doesn't have a certain amount of news value, all the effort in the world won't put it in the newspaper, on television or on radio.*

Generally, three types of stories may come out of your company:

1. *Major News or a Good Human Interest Story.* This could include such events as a major accident, fire, criminal activity, plant shutdown, strike, merger with another company, new plant addition or relocation. Or it could include a good human interest angle such as the blind inspecting flangemeters for the Space Shuttle. This type of story will be done by members of the media instead of your own PR operation. Whether or not the news is favorable to your company, they will give it more space, a better display, prominent headlines, and page 1 or split page (first page of second section) placement. Your expertise in public relations may even be put to the test to counter bad news.

2. *Stories of Lesser News Value,* that are still important may be written either by the media or your own PR operation. Sometimes the media will use a story if it is written by a PR person, but will not assign a staffer because it is not important enough. There is another point to consider. If a story has both regional and statewide appeal, but not a great deal of news value, chances are the story will be used only by the medium cover-

ing it. However, if your PR operation sends a news release to several media, there is a possibility of a few placements. Whether or not they use the news release depends on several factors including the news value, available space, and local interest. Even if they use only the lead of the story, it is worth the price of a stamp to send it. And even if they don't use the release at all, it is helpful to keep the name of your company in front of them. The possibility remains of losing your company's credibility by sending too many news releases. You would do well to make a decision on each news release. If it has local interest only, give it to the local media. If it has broader appeal, mail it to several media outside your local area. A story about something like a new product may be suitable for specialized publications such as the trade press, but lack news value for the general media.

3. *Routine Stories of Marginal News Value* must be written by your company PR operation if they are to see the light of day. They probably would be used only by the local media or in specialized publications.

GETTING ALONG WITH THE MEDIA

You may not believe this, but editors, reporters and news directors are people too. They have families. They eat, drink and sleep. They say "ouch" when they slam their fingers in car doors. And they also are subject to the same temptations and frailties as other people. Consequently, there are some good ones and there are some who are not so good.

However, as a public relations practitioner for your company, you have to deal with all of them. Follow a few rules of common sense and you will get along with your media representatives.

Many people approach the media with the wrong attitude. They feel the media owe them something and should use their organization's news release as a public service. Not so. The prime mission of the media is *to keep the public informed*. With local news, wire services, and news releases inundating them on a daily basis, most media have much more news than they could possibly use with the available space and time. They must constantly decide what has the most news value. If your news release doesn't make it on a particular day, it means they had something more newsworthy or something that had to be published because of the time element. Be patient. If your release has sufficient news value, it will be used.

Newspapers are not entirely heartless, however. They carry their consciences on the editorial page where they are free to publish opinions on the issues of the day, letters from their readers, and various opinionated columns.

When you start thinking of the media as instruments of public service, you might remember that they also are businesses. Like your company, they need to earn a profit or go under. The alternative is government-controlled media.

One of the worst mistakes you can make is to lie to the media. It can do irreparable harm to your relationship with them and destroy your organization's image and credibility. If the media has unfavorable information about your company, it is better to admit it and take your lumps.

Don't get upset if a newspaper rewrites your releases. That's standard operational procedure. Unless the newspaper has completely changed the meaning of a story, your release has accomplished its purpose. It has drawn the attention of the newspaper to your story. Even though your release may be well written, there are several reasons why a newspaper may want to rewrite it. The release may not conform to the newspaper's style. If your release has been sent to several newspapers, the editor may not want the story printed in the exact words used by the other media. The editor may want to use another lead. Or he may want to develop the story beyond its original scope. Is there anything wrong with that? As I have said before, if you can do a better job of writing releases than the media, you are in the wrong business.

Don't stonewall the media if you can possibly avoid it. If you feel that releasing certain information would be damaging to your company, just say, "I would rather not discuss it."

On the other hand, you are not obligated to volunteer any information that would cast your firm in an unfavorable light. Just answer all questions as honestly and as briefly as possible. You don't have to bare your soul to the media.

DEADLINES

Don't approach newspaper reporters with routine stories or questions just before deadline. Although deadline times vary from newspaper to newspaper, morning papers usually close their first editions about midnight and evening papers, about noon. A reporter begins a working day with routine stories. As the deadline for the first edition approaches, the reporter quickens work pace and concentrates on major stories in order to get the latest developments into them. The poorest time to question a reporter about a routine matter is right on deadline. You might even get an abrupt answer. The best time to see a newspaper person is at the beginning of the working day or at the very end (after deadline).

Know the photo and news deadlines of the media with which your company will be dealing. And remember that these deadlines usually apply to major stories, spot news such as fires, bad accidents, criminal activities, obituaries, and other latebreaking stories. Most media would not be able to use your routine company story if they received it close to deadline.

ERRORS AND CORRECTIONS

Doctors make errors. Lawyers make errors. Newspaper, television and radio reporters make errors. The only professionals who don't make mistakes are public relations practitioners and company presidents. It's too bad everyone can't be perfect like us. Just because a reporter is working at top speed trying to get information for six important stories before deadline is no reason for him or her to make an error. Says who?.

In addition to the obvious, there are several reasons why mistakes manage to creep into the print and electronic media, and you can't blame the reporter for all of them. To begin with, when the reporter correctly writes "Jon Johnston" in the copy and it appears in the newspaper as "John Johnson," that is what we call a typographical error. There was a breakdown somewhere in the process between the time it left the VDT or typewriter and the time it appeared in the paper. During my years as a newspaper editor and reporter, I have seen typographical errors after copy has been read by a news editor and a state or city editor, edited by a copy editor, read by a proofreader, and read in the first edition by several reporters.

Sometimes a reporter's source will give him or her the wrong information. A good reporter should attempt to check information if its accuracy is suspicious. However, this is not always possible because of time limitations and other reasons. Sometimes it is better to delete questionable material from a story if it cannot be checked readily.

Along this same line of thinking, let me make another point. A reporter quotes Harry A. Jones, president of International Wombat Corp., as having said, "The world is flat." We all know that statement is false. But, it is news that a person as knowledgeable as Harry Jones said, "The world is flat." The reporter has an obligation to the public to quote him as having made that statement. Of course, the reporter might slip in a line or two about that 1492 voyage after the Jones quote.

With the volume and time limitations, newspapers are remarkably accurate in their handling of news items. Their accuracy should not be compared with magazines, books, and other materials published on different time schedules.

More important than the error is what you or your company do (or don't do) after it appears in the paper. Like other professionals, reporters and editors are sensitive about errors and requests for published corrections. They don't like to have their noses publicly rubbed in their mistakes. The next time the newspaper refers to your firm as the "Colonial Gadget Co." instead of "Colonial Gidget Co.," don't storm into the newsroom brandishing the paper and demanding a retraction or correction at the top of your voice. You may gain something in principle, but you will lose much in media relations.

Some newspapers have a policy of printing corrections and some do not. Those who are reluctant to print corrections feel many errors are of little consequence and do not affect the basic meaning of the stories, and the regular printing of minor corrections would make for dull reading. I would advise you not to ask for a correction unless you believe the error is very damaging to you or your company. If you feel that a correction is really important, ask for it in a quiet, dignified way and take special pains to explain to the editor or reporter why you think so. Sometimes a newspaper will disguise a correction by writing another article with a new lead.

There is another time when you might take action if there is a mistake in a story about your company. If you think the newspaper might use the incorrect information in background material for another story about your company, you might quietly give the reporter the right information without asking for a correction in print.

ADVERTISING

"I just bought a full page of advertising in your

paper. How about a little editorial space?" That is a no-no as far as good media relations is concerned. As a business person, it may be difficult for you to understand why your company is not entitled to a favorable news or feature story after you have paid good dollars for advertising. Despite the fact that advertising is the newspaper's bread and butter, most of the better newspapers do not link paid ads with editorial space. That is because the health of a newspaper depends on circulation, and to gain circulation it must maintain a reputation for fair, unbiased reporting. For that reason, there usually is a sharp division between the business office and editorial departments on the better newspapers. This division becomes a matter of pride with the reporters and editors.

There are exceptions to this rule, of course. Some of the smaller newspapers, including weeklies, may give preferential editorial treatment to advertisers because they feel a certain obligation to support businessmen who support them.

MORE ADVICE

If you don't mind digesting some more advice in the field of media relations, let me throw a few more words of common sense at you. Be polite to the media. Don't try to imitate the hotshot, know-it-all PR flacks you see in the movies or on TV with their feet or hind quarters on an editor's desk. You won't fool anyone.

Also, bear in mind that once you've written and submitted your news release to the media, your job is finished. It's up to the media to decide whether or not they want to use it. *Don't* follow up the release with a telephone call to the reporter or editor to ask if they are going to use it. There is nothing more irritating to a media person than to receive that type of call while working on an important story. If you feel that the story had genuine news value and several days have passed without seeing it in print, you might discreetly inquire only if they have received the release.

I'm sure you have heard those three cute little words, "off the record," so fondly used by worldly politicians. My advice: Don't use them. A reporter isn't talking with you for a social chat. He or she is looking for information to be printed. You're not doing them any favors by giving them information they can't use. And if they should get the same information from another source, they would not be free to use it.

However, if you don't mind if the information appears in print as long as you are not quoted as the source, there is a way of getting around it. You can ask the reporter to attribute the information to a "reliable source" in the story. As head of your company, there is no source more reliable than you. Most reporters will agree to handle the story in this manner.

THE RESOURCE LIST

The Resource List, sometimes called the List of Experts, is another useful public relations tool. If you head a medium-sized business, you probably have people with a great deal of expertise in various fields on your professional staff. Your company may have people with impressive backgrounds in computer sciences, fiscal matters, electronics, physics, engineering, biology, or a multitude of other skills on the payroll. In fact, your vice president may have had extensive dealings with Iranian businessmen and may have broad knowledge of the economy in that country. Or, as a manufacturer of components for the Space Shuttle, your quality control manager would be an ideal source for an educated opinion on a malfunction in that vehicle.

In the course of researching a story, a reporter often encounters questions that call for explanations from experts on the subject. With the Resource List from your company at his disposal, the reporter would be able to call upon a professional from your firm for an opinion.

Your Resource List does not have to be a work of

art. If you have a small company, a photocopied type-written sheet containing the full names, titles, field of expertise, educational background and other quali-fying data, and home and office telephone numbers would do the trick. Or, if your budget can stand it, you could prepare a quality booklet to mail to all the media in your region.

DIRECT MAIL

I have devoted much of this book to methods of reaching the public through the mass media of news-papers, television, radio and magazines. However, there are times when the public can be approached more effectively through direct mail.

The decision of whether or not to use direct mail should be based on your audience. Generally, if you wish to reach a relatively small and specific segment of the public, it is more effective to use direct mail.

For example, if you are in the business of manu-facturing canoes or selling outboard motors, it might be more productive to send brochures to persons in your community who hold fishing licenses. Or, if your small bookstore handles religious literature, you might get better results if your advertising went to church members in the city even though the non-mem-bers may be more in need of it.

If you wish to reach a mass audience, place your message in a newspaper or on the air.

PUBLIC RELATIONS OR ADVERTISING?

There is a degree of confusion between public rela-tions and advertising. Although they have much in common because both are concerned with developing a business reputation, each has its own specialized area and techniques.

Public relations strives to gain the acceptance of the various publics of interest to a business in its rela-tions with customers, suppliers, stockholders, educators, employees and the community. The goal of public relations is good will.

Advertising, on the other hand, is concerned with creating consumer or customer acceptance for the company's products or services. The goal of advertising is sales.

Sometimes these goals will conflict. Advertising might undermine public confidence in the business with copy that exaggerates or that unfairly attacks a competitor. Television and radio commercials and newspaper advertisement might do more harm than good by catering to one group, but offending another segment of society.

By being alert to these possible problems, a competent public relations person can head off situations that might damage the reputation of a business.

CHAPTER

5

5

Photography

There is nothing more trite than the adage, "A picture is worth a thousand words," but it is true. A photo is a perfect device to draw the eye to a story about your business. For that reason, you should include a photo with a news release about your company whenever possible.

Pick up a newspaper or magazine, glance at one page for a few seconds, and put it down. What did you see? Chances are that the only thing you can remember about that page was a picture, the caption, and possibly the headline of the story that went with the picture.

I will not attempt to give you a course in photography, equipment or darkroom procedures because it is beyond the scope of this book. There are many photography magazines and other publications on the market to serve that purpose. But I will offer a few tips to help you work with the media in your public relations photography.

Every release about an individual in your organization should be accompanied by a head and shoulders photo, often called a head shot or one-column cut by the press.

If your story is about a new product, send a photo of that product *in use.* You will have to use your imagination on this one. If your firm is manufacturing flangemeters for the Space Shuttle, maybe you can take a picture of one of your company inspectors giving your product the final okay or a machinist turning one out on a lathe. Send a close-up of the product itself to be used as an inset within the main picture if the photo does not give a good view of the product. However, let me emphasize that the media would be interested only if the product will be used in something newsworthy like the Space Shuttle.

You might also get some media response if your company is introducing a new line of disposable bibs for baboons because of the human interest angle. How about a shot of you as company president tying the first one off the assembly line around the neck of one of our furry cousins at the local zoo? And make sure you identify the participants from left to right.

If your product is something as unexciting as a new type of wood screw, I would skip the general circulation media and concentrate on trade journals. If you are undecided, call your local newspaper. I'm sure the city editor would be glad to give an opinion on the news value of your new product.

As far as the better newspapers are concerned, pictures of check presentations (unless the money is in seven figures), traditional groundbreaking ceremonies, award presentations, ribbon-cuttings, and other antiquated poses staged for PR purposes have gone the way of the nickel beer. If your company has donated money for city playground equipment, show a picture of you pushing a youngster on a swing. The news release about your company giving a scholarship should be accompanied by a head shot of the student recipient. Save the picture of you presenting the award for your company newsletter.

Group pictures also are becoming passé on the pages of the better newspapers. If you have to send a group picture, show them doing something like looking at a map, a blueprint, or a prototype of a new product. Whatever you do, don't pose them in a line against the wall grinning foolishly at the camera. The media call them "firing squad" shots.

While we're discussing group shots, let me give you another tip. *Limit the people in the picture to three.* The layman often considers a news picture to be an instrument to reward people for doing good work. You get something like this: "Joe did a hell of a job designing the flangemeter. He should be in the picture. And don't forget Jake, the machine shop foreman. If it wasn't for Bill, we never would have gotten that government contract. And don't forget Mr. Smith. We've got to get the president in it." And so on . . . and on.

I'm sure they've all done good work and deserve recognition. However, we're trying to get some public relations for the company. If we don't meet professional standards in our PR material, the media are not going to use the picture. There is no point in even taking it to begin with. You can avoid much of that confusion and possible hurt feelings by planning your pictures in advance and having only the subjects on hand when it is taken.

I recall one newspaper photographer who got tired of arguing with organizations about the number of people in a picture. When he was called out on assignment, he would let a bunch of people line up and shoot his flash at them without using film. Then he would proceed to pose two or three people for a picture the way he wanted it. There are some good newspapers and some that are not so good. Unfortunately, some still use firing squad and mass group shots. It makes it that much harder for the ones trying to do a professional job.

HOW TO DO IT

Now that you've had some exposure to the types of photos wanted by the media, the next question is how you are going to get them. You have several options:

Borrow a portrait or head shot from the subject.

Hire a local photographer.

Ask the media to take them.

Take them yourself.

The first option is not very satisfactory. First of all, most people have color portraits of themselves instead of black and white, which the media prefer for reproduction. Color prints can be reproduced, but the quality is not as good as black and white. Second, most people only have one picture of themselves and you can send a photo to only one newspaper. Thirdly, you have to worry about getting the portrait back to its owner.

There is nothing wrong with hiring a professional photographer if you have a few bucks in your public relations budget. Most communities have such a person who makes a living by taking wedding pictures, doing free-lance work for the local newspaper and other publications, and commercial photography. The only drawback is that the negatives are the property of the photographer and you must pay for the print every time you want one.

If your story is of a major nature, you won't have any trouble getting the media to take their own pictures. In fact, they would rather take their own because they have more control over the quality.

Picture policies vary from paper to paper. Some seldom touch public relations offerings while others are more generous. If the story is of a routine nature, you may have difficulty in getting picture coverage by the media. Sometimes if the subject of the story will go to the newspaper's photography department, they will take a head shot to go with the story.

In the long run, taking your own pictures is the

most productive and least expensive system providing you or the person who does your PR has enough time.

Let's start with the head shot which you will use more than any other to accompany releases about new company personnel, promotions, awards, and other recognition stories. Find a spot in your plant or office where you have a soft northern light coming through a window. Unless you have a set of lights, it is better to use existing light with a fast black and white film such as Kodak Tri-X pan, ISO 400. If you are not adept at bouncing light off the ceiling, you are likely to wash out the features of the individual with your flash attachment. You will retain character lines and soft shadows on the face with existing light.

Hang a white sheet from a frame to provide a neutral or bland background. A busy background detracts from the subject. Find two stools about the same height and seat your subject facing the window. Use a tripod if you have one. Most amateur photographers have a tendency to shake the camera slightly when they press the shutter. This creates a blurring effect on the negative and the picture appears to be out of focus. If you don't have a tripod, you can make a tripod of your body by tucking your elbows tightly into your sides like marksmen do in Olympic rifle competition.

Have your subject turn slightly counterclockwise and then look back at you over his right shoulder. If one side of his face is too dark, an assistant out of camera range with a large piece of white paper or cardboard can reflect light from the window onto the dark side of his face to get the desired effect. Sit on the other stool with your 35mm single-lens reflex camera at the same level as your subject's face.

Get close enough to the subject so his head and shoulders almost fill the picture area. Focus the camera on the pupils of the eyes and then turn the camera to provide a vertical format. You may have to ask the subject to move his chin up or down. Take some with him looking directly into the camera and others looking over your right shoulder. Portrait photographers try to make a perfect oval of the face of the subject. Take a whole roll of film so you will have a wide choice when you make up your contact prints or proofs.

Involve the subject in the selection process if that is possible. Some people are very sensitive about their pictures, especially those who are not particularly photogenic. Try as you will, you will not be able to get a picture that will satisfy them. In that case, encourage them to get black and white pictures made by a professional portrait photographer at their own expense. Most people will be glad to pay the cost because they like to see their pictures in the newspaper.

When you are using your flash attachment, try to keep your subjects away from walls because the flash will cast a big shadow behind them. You can avoid this by bouncing your light off the ceiling.

Taking pictures in direct sunlight also is difficult because it creates a blotchy effect. Try to get your subjects in a more subdued light.

Have you ever been to a sports event or other function in a large auditorium and seen hundreds of flashes winking at you from the third row bleachers? This has never ceased to amuse me. Presumably the bleacher-based photographers are aiming their picture boxes at the action below. Their electronic flashes at that distance are about as effective as a flashlight in trying to spot airplanes at night.

THE DARKROOM

If you can bake a cake, you can set up and operate your own darkroom. Developing and printing black and white film is not as complicated as some would have you think. It is just a matter of correct quantities, temperatures, and timing. And, in addition to the media, it would be useful in preparing photos for company publications and other purposes.

You will need a room a little larger than a telephone booth without windows. Plumbing within the darkroom would be very helpful but it is not absolutely essential. If there are any light leaks after you close the door, you will have to nail a strip around the door to provide absolute darkness. Counters and shelves around three walls of the darkroom also would be helpful.

The enlarger for printing is the most expensive item in your darkroom equipment. You could probably pick up a usable one for less than $200. Other darkroom needs include a timer, photo paper, an easel to hold your photo paper, a printing light, a small tank with reels to develop film, a thermometer, trays, chemicals, and a few other sundry items. If you have a large mailing list, you may prefer a stabilizer which allows you to print many photos quickly.

If you would rather not develop and print your own film, you still have other options. You could send them to a pharmacy or photography shop for processing. However, that involves the drawback of having to wait a few days for the prints. And the story may lose its news value by that time. Some newspapers will process a roll of film you take if they want to use the story. But, again, you would be limiting your release to one newspaper.

PHOTO CAPTIONS

Write your photo captions or cutlines as they are called in the profession on the same letterhead paper that you use for news releases. Identify them as photo captions or cutlines. The captions should contain the full names of the people in the picture, titles, identification from left to right, when and where the action took place, and an explanation of the action. Sometimes the caption will have a photographer's credit line in parenthesis in the following manner: (Photo by Smith). Some PR people like to paste captions to the back of photos. Memories of a city editor trying to peel paper from a photo and muttering, "Why do they paste them?" are still vivid in my mind. I prefer to fold a caption and insert the photo inside it. If a caption is written properly, there is little chance of confusing it with the wrong photo, even if there are two photos with a release.

MAILING PHOTOS

Photos that are 5 by 7 inches in size seem to be generally accepted by the media. They also are more convenient to handle and are not as expensive as the 8- by 10-inch photo paper. Mail them with your news release, caption, and a cardboard reinforcement. A "Photo Enclosed" stamp to mark the outside of the envelope hopefully adds further protection to your photo.

If you have a large mailing list, you may want to use a photo availability notice instead of sending photos to all the newspapers. One method is to reproduce a print on your photocopy machine and mail it with the caption and a notice that a print is available on request.

CHAPTER

6

6

Maintaining Good
Community Relations

Benjamin Franklin was a scientist, philosopher, publisher and one of the fathers of the republic. However, few would consider him one of the first practitioners of successful community relations. In fact, the term, community relations, much less the profession of public relations, was not even known when Franklin was operating his small Philadelphia printing shop in the early 1730s.

Yet, as his *Poor Richard's Almanac* and *The Pennsylvania Gazette* were becoming the most widely-read publications in America, he was also making a name for himself as Philadelphia's first citizen. Franklin's public-spirited civic activities probably were the ultimate example of community relations. His work should serve as a model for all businessmen who wish to generate good will for their company. There is no question that his extensive use of the marketing tool of public relations in his community relations efforts gave a tremendous boost to his small printing business.

Although Franklin was only a businessman and private citizen most of the time, he almost turned Philadelphia upside down by spearheading many civic improvements. He established the first public library in America, organized a fire department, started a fire insurance company, arranged for street lighting, defended the freedom of the press, founded a hospital, was chief founder of the college that became the University of Pennsylvania, and was involved in the addition of science courses to the Latin and Greek of other colleges' curricula. Respected by all, Franklin often was asked to mediate arguments.

The versatile printer also extended his influence beyond the City of Philadelphia. With his enthusiasm and organizational skills, he improved the mail service throughout the colonies and was selected to be postmaster-general.

Franklin also was one of the first to understand that the 13 colonies should learn to think of themselves as one country. His achievements went on and on from the New World to the European countries of England and France.

How about it, Mr. company president? Doesn't Benjamin Franklin inspire you to do great things and earn good will for your firm throughout the community and beyond?

As you can probably guess at this point, the key to good community relations is simply being a good citizen like Franklin. If your only interest in the community is what you can get out of it, you would do well to reconsider your own philosophy and company policies. You have to accept civic responsibility and take an active interest in the well-being of your community in order to reap the long-range benefits of good will toward your company.

Your company could take the following steps in the interests of community relations:

    1. Take an active interest in community problems and help to solve them.

2. Sponsor youth activities.
3. Take part in local government.
4. Participate actively in business and service groups.
5. When possible, purchase your supplies and materials from local companies.
6. Take part in civic activities.
7. Encourage community education and culture.
8. Let community organizations use your plant for meetings.
9. Support local charity drives.

I'm sure you can think of a few more activities to help to establish you and your business as an asset to the community.

Good community relations are a necessary part of the public relations effort for both large and small business concerns. John C. Aspley (1961) gives several examples of firms of varying sizes which have exerted tremendous influence over their respective communities. In 1955, Ford Motor Co. opened a new assembly plant in Milpitas, California, a small municipality on San Francisco Bay. The rapid influx of employees resulted in the construction of 1,000 new homes. Local facilities were inadequate and the town was in financial difficulty. Ford encouraged the town to incorporate as a city and then loaned money to the municipality until the tax money began to roll in. Within two years, the sleepy little town was transformed into a vibrant community.

General Motors also has an active community relations effort. One program designed to spread good will throughout the community was the General Motors Film Library. In 1950, more than 16 million people viewed films produced to "help build a better understanding of GM as an institution, its forward-looking policies, the superiority of its products, the quality of its personnel, its research, its facilities, and its know-how."

Richard D. Edwards, owner of a small store in Lansford, Pennsylvania, had his own special method of generating good will. Remembering his late mother's advice that flowers should be given to the living, on Mothers Day, 1939, he invited 15 mothers from the community to a party. He fed, entertained, and gave them the flowers that his mother had suggested. Edwards continued the Mothers Day parties for years. At one party, he served 348 mothers ranging in age from 70 to 94.

Dwayne Walton, president of Concorde Supermarkets, really got into the meat of his community relations program. Nineteen-year-old Cindy Temp of Coon Valley, Wisconsin, produced a champion steer in 1985 and sold it for $107,930, or $86 a pound to Cub Foods of Onalaska, Wisconsin. Walton, owner of the local Cub Foods store, said "We bought the steer because we wanted to show our support for the county fair and the 4-H program, as well as the farming community. We have been very successful with our business in the area and we wanted to put something back into the community." The steer was later donated to a charity in the community. The Temp family said the money would help put their six children through college.

Tom Mahoney and Rita Hession (1949) cite the example of Rich's of Atlanta, Georgia, which launched a series of public service programs and increased sales at more than double the rate for department stores in general. When Atlanta used up all the money earmarked for paying teachers during the 1930 Christmas season, the store cashed city checks post-dated to the next January without requiring that teachers buy anything. The store also helped the City of Atlanta with financial problems during the depression years, with its grief after 121 persons died in a 1946 hotel fire, gave free newspapers to hospital patients, presented awards to high school and college students, and 4-H Club prize winners, and sponsored full-page advertisements extolling the glories of the State of Georgia.

Executives of Rich's also participated in many

civic activities. Walter Rich, one of the store presidents, was a member of both city and state school
boards, supported Atlanta orchestras and operas,
contributed to many charities and left bequests to or-
phanages, hospitals, and colleges, including some institutions for blacks. And, let me remind you, this was
in the Deep South well before the civil rights movement
of the 1960s.

The Rich Foundation, which handles the store's
philanthropy, gave Emory University a $250,000 busi-
ness administration building known as the Rich Memorial Building. The grant included funds for 10 years
of maintenance. The foundation also has given the city
and country schools an FM broadcasting station for
educational programs. The City College of New York
presented a national award in 1947 to Rich's for a series
of radio programs devoted to Georgia history and
resources.

At an anniversary of the store, a president of the
Georgia Power Co. said, "In all Atlanta there is not a
single human being who speaks ill of Rich's and none
who does not rejoice in its success." Can you beat that
for good community relations?

THE COMPANY AND THE COMMUNITY

The relationship between your company and the
community should be mutually beneficial. The company provides steady work for the people and, in return,
the people should support the company by helping to
hold down production costs without sacrificing the
quality of the product or service. The community support could include transportation facilities; power,
fuel, and water supplies; available housing and plant
sites; educational, recreational, religious, and cultural
facilities; understanding, respect, and fair treatment
from the community's public servants in such areas as
courts, taxes, and law enforcement; helping to reduce
excessive costs of operation; and loyalty by speaking
well of the company.

You and your company should accept the responsibility of civic leadership. If you or one of your company employees rolls up his sleeves and pitches in when a community development project such as a new park or a youth center is proposed, you can find no better public relations.

It is also important that you do more than just lend your name to a United Way or March of Dimes campaign. Your contribution will be more obvious and appreciated if you become personally involved in the drive. Don't be afraid to organize a group of volunteers or swing a brush cutter to clear land for a town recreation area.

You shouldn't be the only representative of your company who is involved in community relations. Whether you have two employees or many, you should counsel them on the value of public relations. There are countless courtesies they can extend to the public that will make a lasting impression. If your firm operates two, three, or a fleet of vehicles, advise your drivers to practice good manners with other motorists and offer assistance when needed. The public will judge your company by the actions of your employees in the community. It goes without saying that your customers should be treated like royalty. All visitors to your plant, even salesmen from whom you do not intend to buy anything, should be handled with the utmost courtesy. And good manners in answering your plant telephone is another important consideration.

Above all, determine what your employees think of you. Do they badmouth you and the company at the local bar, general store or Saturday night poker game? That is bad. You may have a morale problem that will undermine community relations. Get to the heart of the problem. Discuss the matter with your company officers, supervisors, foremen, union officials, the plant custodian, or anyone who is close to the employees. Erect a complaint box. Maintain an open-door policy to your office. Take an active interest in your employees and their families.

The problem may be simpler than you think and easily remedied. Or it may be a bit more complex. If it is a money problem and there is nothing that can be done about it, at least call a meeting to explain in detail the need to hold down production costs and maintain a profit margin to keep the plant in operation. You may be pleasantly surprised by the quality of the solutions suggested by your employees. After all, they have as much a stake in the future of the company as you and it is to their benefit as well to hold down production costs.

Another way of involving your employees in public relations is to post opportunities for community service in company publications such as the monthly newsletter, on bulletin boards, or in other areas where they can be seen. You could also recognize employees who are helping the community.

AN IDEA LIST

Now that we understand the general concept of community relations, let's have some specific ideas on what we can do to project a favorable image of our company to the public:

1. Volunteer yourself or appoint one of your company officials to help promote and develop a civic program such as a charity drive, a fair, or an auction.

2. Name one of your company executives who speaks well or give a talk yourself to the chamber of commerce, service clubs, civic associations, or other groups.

3. Provide jobs for the handicapped, aged, or mentally retarded. Make sure the public knows of your action, but don't overdo the publicity. Use a subtle approach to disseminate the information. (The blind are inspecting flangemeters for the Space Shuttle.)

4. Conduct a Christmas party for the children of your employees and their friends.

5. Hold an open house with demonstrations and exhibits at your plant. Ask employees to invite their friends and neighbors.

6. Encourage officials of your company to hold active membership in service clubs, religious, and fraternal organizations.

7. Invite youth organizations, service clubs, women's clubs, and other community groups to tour your plant. Offer them refreshments.

8. Establish something at your plant that will make your company a landmark. These can include beautiful gardens, a striking sculpture, a large clock, an antique snowplow, or a herd of llamas. (The Bostitch Division of Textron, Inc. maintains beautifully landscaped lawns and pools inhabited by hundreds of geese at its East Greenwich, Rhode Island, plant.)

9. As head of your company,.get involved in some social betterment program. Make sure the media know about it.

10. Establish a speakers bureau to provide information about your company to educational, civic, social and service groups.

11. Prepare a video tape about your company, product or service to be loaned to various organizations in your community.

12. Compile a mailing list to distribute company brochures, newsletters, articles, and other materials to civic and government leaders in your community.

13. Arrange for you or one of your company executives to appear on television or radio talk shows.

14. Prepare a series of newspaper advertisements to inform the community about important activities at your plant.

15. Maintain constant media relations to keep them informed about what's going on at your company.

PUBLIC SERVICE

Although there was probably more room for civic improvement when this nation was young, there are still many opportunities for your company's public service projects. Look around. Take a drive down the road. Maybe the sides of the highway are littered with beer cans, bottles, papers, and other trash. Why not organize a group of your employee's children and some company trucks for a "Clean-up Day" or a "Beautify the City" project? Maybe you have collected some weird-looking trash in your program. Great! Pile it up as high as you can and create one of those modernistic sculptures. Then invite television and newspaper photographers to aim their cameras at your work of art. Get in the picture yourself by applying the finishing touches to your masterpiece.

Is your firm located in a state with a returnable bottle law? If so, cash in your beer and soda cans and bottles at the redemption center. You don't have to be a professional practitioner to know what to do with the money, do you? Give it to a highly visible charity, of course. That's public relations! And make sure the media know about it.

Does your company own any undeveloped land which is accessible to the community? Why not mobilize the employees and children again? Clear out the heavy underbrush, build some picnic tables and fireplaces, and open it to the public as a recreation area. And don't forget to erect the sign reading: "Community Picnic Grounds. Compliments of Colonial Gidget Co."

Do you need another public service project? Check with the recreation director at a nursing home in your community. Offer the services of your employees to bring a little cheer to the older set. They may welcome some entertainment from talented members of your company. Maybe someone could build a few planters to set outside their windows. If possible, try to involve residents of the home in any projects that you initiate.

It is important that they feel useful. Match the interests of your employees with persons in the nursing home. They may, more than anything else, enjoy a chat with someone.

I'm sure you can find many other public service projects in your community. You can launch them on a large or small scale, depending on the size of your company and available resources.

Your company could sponsor a Little League team and you could volunteer to be a coach or umpire. You and a couple of employees could clean up an old cemetery that is overgrown with brush and repair broken gravestones. Sponsor a Boy, Girl, Cub Scout, or Brownie Troop and volunteer to lead them.

There is no end to the possibilities. Some areas to consider as you start your thought process are: community improvement, working with the handicapped, improving roads, flood prevention, school and college projects, safety, fire and accident prevention, health and sanitation, and good citizen projects.

MEMBERSHIPS

To the entrepreneur, membership in service clubs, professional organizations, trade and technical associations, employers' and manufacturers' associations, civic clubs and social clubs are a necessary part of the public relations effort. However, initiation fees, dues and other expenses connected with these memberships may become an increasing financial burden, especially if you are the owner of a newly-formed or small business. If your company also picks up the tab for several top executives who have joined various organizations, then your public relations budget may be under a severe strain. For that reason, you may have to be more selective in choosing the clubs and associations to carry your name and those of your executives on their membership rolls.

One way to choose the right organization is to check the members. Do the president of the bank, the mayor, the superintendent of schools, the head administrator of the hospital, the president of the college, the chairman of the board of the major industry in the community, and top businessmen belong to the Rotary or the Kiwanis Clubs? If most are members of the Rotary Club, you might do well to cast your lot with them.

Joining organizations also is an explicit marketing tactic. So choose the groups that contain customers of your company.

Another way to get more mileage out of your public relations budget is to require your executives (including yourself) to pay at least a portion of the expenses involved in these memberships out of their own pockets. This should be agreeable to officials of your company because they would be advancing their own careers as well as the public relations effort. You could also require executives to attend a certain percentage of club meetings and be involved in committee activity if they wish the company to pay their way.

Don't underestimate the public relations value of these memberships, however. Rubbing shoulders with community leaders and getting to know them on a first-name basis is an essential part of the good will process for your company.

SERVICE AND CIVIC CLUBS

You will get out of service clubs what you put into them. Most groups like the Kiwanis, Rotary and Lions Clubs have varied civic betterment or social relations projects which can serve the community relations function that you should establish for your company. Even if you only attend a luncheon meeting, you will meet important people whose friendships will prove to be valuable in the future.

From a public relations standpoint, the most important local civic organization is the chamber of commerce. However, the effectiveness of a chamber hinges on its leaders. If the heads of the group are enthusiastic, interested in their community, and implement creative ideas into worthwhile civic improvement programs, they can do great good for the municipality. Unfortunately, some chambers of commerce are controlled by special interests such as downtown merchants who might promote their own interests at the expense of suburban shopping centers, push a favorite transportation project, or work for parallel parking on Main Street.

THE EDUCATIONAL SIDE

A businessman who works with schools and colleges makes an investment in the future while spreading good will in his community. The students of today will be the community leaders of tomorrow.

Fred Boucher, a proprietor of Fred's Vending Service of Waterville, Maine, shows one example of how a small businessman can generate good will for his firm as well as support education. He offers scholarships to students who have displayed entrepreneurial talents at Thomas College, a local business school. He also reaps the benefits of the college public relations program when news releases about the entrepreneurial scholarships are sent to the hometown media of the student recipients. One award recipient devised a series of computer games. Another established her own successful ice cream business.

In addition to scholarships, you can provide assistance to educational institutions through outright grants, special purpose contributions, lecturers, and donations of video tapes and informational materials. However, you should be careful not to give literature that promotes a specific product.

PUBLIC RELATIONS AND RELIGION

Regardless of your faith, you can generate good will for your company through the religious community. But do it in a quiet manner. Pillars of the church are often community leaders. Your contribution will not go unnoticed.

Maybe the church or synagogue is conducting a fund-raising or building program. Offer the expertise of your company. I'm sure they could use your company accountant to handle the finances. If you are an architect, a building contractor, a plumber, or an electrician, there is no question that your services would be appreciated. As head of your company, you have solid management ability that could be applied to the project. If you are the owner of a printing firm, donate the campaign brochures. Or maybe you have firsthand fund-raising experience.

John C. Aspley (1961) cites the case of a Rock Island, Illinois, merchant who launched a successful good will program at Rothchild's Department Store. The manager decided to conduct a free coffee hour, but was faced with the problem of how to provide service. Finally, he came up with the idea of offering to pay $125 to any churchwomen's organization or charitable group that would do that chore. The system worked out well and for a total cost of $200 a month he secured the good will of both his customers and many organizations in Rock Island and adjacent Moline and Davenport. And consider his savings in labor costs.

A simple donation to a religious institution may start the good will mechanism rolling in the minds of the community. And, don't forget, such financial contributions are tax deductible.

Make friends of the clergymen in your community. The good will and cooperation of church leaders is a valuable asset to your company. They are usually articulate and help to influence public opinion.

OPEN HOUSE

An open house at your plant can serve many purposes. A valuable community relations tool, such a function can show community leaders, others in the same business, the trade and local media, stockholders customers, dealers, suppliers, employees and their families, and even the general public how your company operates. They attain a sense of identification with your business after attending an event of that nature. This is especially true if it involves a tour of your facilities. For that reason, many firms sponsor tours of their plants and open houses.

An open house can give you an opportunity to demonstrate to consumers that your product is made from quality materials. Families of employees can see that the breadwinner has excellent working conditions. You can show your stockholders that their money is being invested wisely with modern equipment and manufacturing techniques. Students can observe the advantages and career opportunities at your company. And the general public will be able to determine that your new company will be an asset to the community.

You should start planning your open house well in advance of the date. Six months is not too long for a major event. One of the first decisions you should make is the purpose of the open house. You may want to promote community relations, show off a new plant to the media, demonstrate how your product is made, or inspire employee loyalty.

When you have pinpointed the reason for the open house, you should plan every detail of the event to emphasize this objective. For example, if you have community relations in mind, you should invite all the important people in the area and those living in the immediate vicinity of the plant. And, of course, if the open house is a media event, invite all newspapers, television and radio stations and the trade press. And don't forget to display some visual object such as an exhibit of your product for television.

You should name one person, preferably a top executive, to head the open house committee. Appoint a person who has the authority and drive to get the program off the ground. Other members of the committee should be assigned to various functions in accordance with their expertise. Try to involve all sections or departments of your plant in the preparation, including the union.

Before you set the date for your open house, it is a good idea to determine if other local events are scheduled for the same day to avoid possible conflicts. Steer clear of holidays and religious observances. Set the time for early enough in the day to allow your visitors an opportunity to register, hear the welcoming address, take the tour, ask questions, and have refreshments.

If you are operating with a limited budget, you will have to plan the open house in accordance with that spending plan. Try to estimate the size of the crowd if it is open to the general public. You might check the attendance figures at similar functions in the past. Make sure you cover all expenses including refreshments or a caterer, publicity, press kits, name cards for identification, company histories, programs, entertainment, invitations and postage, custodial help, overtime, parking lot attendants, police officers, decorations, exhibits, prizes, favors, samples, signs, supplies and other costs.

Be sure you have enough parking space and chairs if you plan an assembly program. If you anticipate a number of young children in the crowd, you might set up a nursery attended by an employee. Sometimes it is helpful to have a public address system to announce beginnings of various exhibits, demonstrations, events, and other messages. Check the restrooms to make sure they are clean, clearly marked and well stocked. If a musical group is part of the entertainment, provide a room for them to store their instrument cases and other equipment.

Often it is helpful to have a rehearsal or dry run before the open house to spot unforeseen snags and problems, and coordinate the time.

Mail your invitations at least two weeks in advance. In addition to inviting newspapers, television and radio stations and representatives of trade newspapers or magazines, you might insert paid advertisements in the media and display posters if the event is open to the general public. Some companies provide a photographer in case the media want a picture of a portion of the program. Provide a press kit for each media representative with background material and such information as quarterly and annual company reports. Include picture order cards in case they wish photos of company executives, products or services in use, and the plant.

After the open house, follow through with a critique as soon as possible to judge its success, obtain ideas for a similar event in the future, and avoid problems in the next open house. Comments and suggestions by visitors should be considered. It is good internal public relations to write "thank you" notes to those who worked on the open house.

PLANT VISITORS

Guided tours or visits are more important to some companies than others. For a firm whose product goes directly to the consumer like a meat packing or auto assembly plant, it is good public relations to demonstrate the clean and efficient working conditions.

Probably one of the more impressive plant tours is offered by the Anheuser-Busch beer company at Busch Gardens in Tampa, Florida. As a visitor to the plant, I rode an overhead monorail and viewed exotic animals in delightful settings landscaped like their natural habitats. Nowhere did I see cages or similar cramped quarters like those maintained in traditional zoos.

After the monorail trip, a guide led our party on a narrated tour through the plant to see the brewing process. At the conclusion of the tour, the visitors were given free samples of the company's product.

Another memorable tour is conducted by The Jack Daniel Distillery of Lynchburg, Tennessee, which has been named to the National Register of Historic Places. Visitors are taken through the entire distillation process. They see corn, rye and barley malt ground and mixed with pure iron-free spring water, fermented, smoothed out with the age-old charcoal mellowing process, placed in barrels, and sent to a warehouse to age.

Established in 1866, the distillery is the oldest registered one in the United States. The distillery widely distributes an attractive brochure containing photos, a map and an invitation welcoming visitors to Jack Daniel Hollow to see how the sour mash Tennessee whiskey is made. That is how to do public relations.

In planning tours of your own plant, make sure that the point where the tour begins is attractive and interesting. That is where the visitor forms his first impression of the plant. You might hang a map or chart showing the layout of the plant and the various operations in the manufacturing process. A receptionist should greet the visitors immediately as they enter the plant.

Some of the larger companies train guides to answer questions and take visitors on a tour through the company building. You might recruit them from among your employees. Tour guides should have a pleasant personality and a good disposition, and be articulate, neat in appearance, and patient.

Like the open house, a tour should have a specific objective. That could range from how the product is made to how it serves the public. Without an objective, the visitor could leave the plant in a state of confusion. Some companies show visitors a film before the tour begins or emphasize the tour theme with a short talk.

Plant tours are an excellent publicity tool for your company. Visits by interesting groups or people from other countries provide good material for photos and stories. Invite the media to your plant on the day the tour is scheduled or, if they have other commitments, you might send them a news release and picture.

EXHIBITS

You can generate public relations for your company by entering an exhibit of your product or service in a county fair, trade show or convention. If possible, get some motion into your exhibit to help attract the casual observer. Show your product at work. For example, if your company manufactures water pumps, show your product doing its thing with a tank of water. Use your imagination in creating your exhibit. Maybe you could provide an illustration of a ground well behind your pump.

If your company manufactures motorcycles like Soichiro Honda, you might devise a continuously moving background of countryside behind your machine with an electric motor to give the illusion it is moving along a road.

You should staff your exhibit at all times while the fair or show is open. If you can't be present yourself, make sure the person is fully qualified to answer questions about your product or service.

Keep your exhibit simple. If you make it too complex, you may lose your audience. Plan the exhibit so it will make an impression on those who hurry by as well as those who stop to read. They call this "billboard value." Have brochures or promotional literature available to give the public something that will make an impression after they leave your exhibit and something they can read at their leisure.

Sometimes exhibitors distribute free souvenirs or novelties at their booths. However, be selective about giving them to a person who is truly interested in your product or service. Such items are expensive and there is much waste in their distribution.

Events such as fairs, conventions, or trade shows provide an excellent opportunity to determine what the public thinks of your company, service or product. This can be obtained by having questionnaires available at your booth. You might tie them in with a drawing or a prize. Polling techniques or sampling public opinion will be covered more fully in Chapter 11.

CUSTOMER RELATIONS

Did you ever walk into a store to buy some merchandise and have the shopkeeper say, "If I were you, I would buy a gooflinger at (local discount house). All you are paying for here is the big brand name. They have ones just as good for half the price."? That gave you a nice warm feeling, didn't it? The shopkeeper may have lost that particular sale, but she made a good customer for life. You will trade at that store again and again. What you have experienced is a public relations practice called "good customer relations."

If your firm is a retail outlet or one that deals directly with the public, you would do well to choose your employees carefully. They should have pleasant personalities and be well-liked by those they meet. In addition, they should understand the importance of good will to your business. This should apply not only to the sales personnel, but to the dealers and the servicing staff. Those who distribute your company's product or services have an opportunity to make good friends for your firm as well as establish their own prestige and position in the community. However, it is up to you as head of the company to conduct a training program.

Your employees should know how to do their job well in order to inspire public confidence in the company and minimize reasons for complaints. They should be public relations conscious, courteous at all times, and cognizant of the benefits of good will.

To keep your employees well satisfied, you should provide a pay plan with incentives, job security, opportunities for promotion, good working conditions, and the right tools. And, like the storekeeper in the gooflinger case, they should be well-versed in practical psychology.

The good traveling salesperson also is an expert in customer relations. In fact, constant contact with customers and prospects adds a great deal to the effectiveness of your public relations program. An active salesperson spends days in continuous conversation with people from all walks of life. They love to tell stories and jokes. So why not provide a few stories that will generate public relations for the company and watch his smoke?

Salespeople also are experts at making friends with customers and everyone else for that matter. There is no question that buyers in a competitive market give their orders to the salespeople they like.

There are ways of improving customer relations within your plant, as well. The reception desk, which deals with a considerable number of people during the course of a year, is an important part of your company. The person who sits behind it should be well-trained in dealing with the public and cognizant of the public relations aspect of the job. Some companies give this position to salespeople who have reached retirement age because they usually are outgoing, public relations-minded and good conversationists.

Visiting salesmen from suppliers also are an excellent public relations medium. If they receive intelligent cooperation from the receptionist in helping them to see the right person, they will speak favorably of your company.

The telephone operator at your firm's switchboard also helps to project a favorable image of your company to customers and other callers. Telephone operators should practice good telephone manners, voice modulation, and how to handle special situations. Instruct them to deliver a cheery greeting in answering incoming calls.

Sales executives are becoming more and more conscious of the value of good customer relations in the public relations effort. Surveys have shown that more customers are lost through discourteous treatment, poor service, or indifference than for any other reasons.

The telephone operator who answers a call, the

clerk who takes the order, the driver who makes the delivery, and any other person who has direct contact with the public all influence opinion for or against your company.

Want to test the quality of customer relations in your firm? You don't have to be too sneaky about it. Just telephone your company and ask to speak to one of your executives. See how you are greeted by the operator and how long you have to wait to talk to the executive.

PERSON-TO-PERSON

The value of person-to-person contact cannot be overemphasized in the public relations process. You should encourage all employees of your company from the top executives to the custodial staff to speak about your firm in glowing, enthusiastic terms at every opportunity, especially when they are talking to non-employees in the community. This may sound like trite advice. But, when you stop to think about it, such a practice makes a good deal of sense. All your employees have a stake in the welfare of your company. This word-of-mouth publicity is a necessary ingredient of the public relations mix. When your company does well on the marketplace and the bottom line gets fatter and fatter, the paychecks of your employees will get fatter and fatter. Emphasize this point to your employees at every opportunity. And, by all means, follow through on your promise.

Companies have a habit of overestimating the power of the written word. They assume that all their employees and all publics read company publications and print media from the first to the last page. That is not completely true. There are many that read only selected items and the headlines, and look at the pictures. That is why we must talk to people as well as provide written material. And talk is less expensive.

WINNING COMMUNITY ACCEPTANCE

I'm sure you can remember the turbulent 60s when

anything — and any business — that smacked of being part of the "establishment" was the "enemy" to many young people. Now, in the middle 80s, a lot of those same young people are entrepreneurs like yourself and are trying to win acceptance in the community. They don't consider themselves to be the "enemy."

Of course, there are — and there always will be — those on the extreme left end of the political spectrum who will never be satisfied until a completely socialistic (or communistic) form of government owns all property, business, and utilities. They will continue to work for the overthrow of capitalism, the establishment of a communist society based on labor and not profit, and the establishment of a workers' and farmers' government.

For that reason, we must continue our educational campaign to counteract the philosophy of production for use rather than production for profit. This effort will take more than just an occasional news release to the press.

Winning public acceptance for business calls for a carefully considered public relations policy and the aggressive implementation of that policy, a continuous well-planned community relations program, and full management and financial support.

Such a program must touch the depths of human relationships, be fundamentally sound, courageous, capture the community's fancy, and have a great deal of news value. The program also must be important to the community. The success of the program may be measured by the question: How well does it benefit the community?

I would also like to make another point. If the program serves the employees of your company well, it will also benefit the community because your workers are part of the community. Helping to make the community a better place in which to live and raising the cultural level of the community benefits both your employees and the community as a whole. However, it would be well to approach your community relations campaign in a subtle manner so it will not appear to be just a publicity stunt by the company.

If your company succeeds in obtaining the good will of the community, you will also make a contribution to nourishing the good will of the American people as a whole for the private enterprise system. In fact, if each firm in every community in the United States did its part in the process of building a good will program, the effect would be a tremendous help in the problem of creating more acceptance for the private-enterprise system.

ECONOMIC EDUCATION

In keeping with our program to generate public support for the free-enterprise system, we might initiate an economic education campaign. You could explore several factors in planning such a program. They could include the reasons people want to work such as money, job satisfaction, ambition, self-improvement, security and challenge.

In recent years, the development of robotics, data processing systems, and other forms of automation have eliminated some of the negative aspects of work such as repetition and monotony. Of course, they have also caused other problems such as unemployment that have made necessary job retraining programs. On occasion, workers have expressed a yearning to return to the days of master craftmanship instead of mass production and distribution. However, they are unwilling to return to that standard of living that goes with that system of production.

In order to be successful, the economic education program cannot be accomplished by your company alone. It must begin at the top management level and work downward through middle management to the workers in every plant, mill, office, mine or organization. Such a program probably could be spearheaded by a trade association, professional society, or a group of companies.

For example, the electric power industry could conduct a series of public relations workshops to educate several companies in one region on methods of reaching the community. In addition to emphasizing the need for greater support for the free-enterprise system, these workshops also could cover such subjects as proper insulation of homes, factories, plants and business offices; conservation of electricity; public appreciation of electrical power; a better understanding of the cost and price structure of electricity and the industry's economic and financial needs; the investment of money in industry stocks; the fundamentals of generating electricity and the role of electricity in the future.

Armed with this information, the various electric companies could carry the campaign to the community level. The power firms could include brochures with their electric bills, develop promotional materials, conduct open houses and demonstrations, send news releases to the media and provide speakers for community groups.

John C. Aspley (1961) cites another approach to economic education. A series of "town meetings" could be staged with a debate, open discussion or meetings with speakers.

A company in a one-plant community outside of Chicago sponsored lectures by six nationally-known speakers in a series of six town meetings held in a school auditorium. Each speaker discussed one area of the economic situation from the standpoint of the community.

A similar program was conducted by several service clubs in Evansville, Indiana.

Various types of economic education programs can be conducted at your plant. You may want to employ an outside organization with expertise on the college or university level. This type of program would meet the approval of top management because the discussion leader would not be a "company man." It would equip middle management to train supervisors to discuss economic problems with those they supervise. And rank-and-file employees could take advantage of this program on a voluntary discussion-group basis.

The company could provide another type of economic education program by buying instructional materials and training supervisors or members of the personnel department as discussion leaders. This program could then be made available to various community organizations.

Although the outside-expertise program is expensive, it is more effective because it avoids possible criticism as "company propaganda." The propaganda issue may be a problem in some cases, while it makes no difference in others.

Some economic education programs may fail because the approach is obviously company propaganda. When your company sets out to educate the public about the advantages of the free enterprise system in America, keep in mind that the campaign will succeed only if a certain amount of trust exists. This trust may be nurtured by presenting the facts in as interesting and understandable a way as possible.

Most people are influenced by the psychological aspects of any problem they may be considering and the project should be introduced from the angle of the individual's self-interest. They object more to the manner in which they are treated than to the end result of the treatment. Our basic failure in human relations has been in the area of human contact. People want to feel that there is genuine concern by the company for their welfare and the company wants to feel that it has the loyalty and respect of its employees and the community.

If the company is successful in its campaign, people turn to the firm for the products and services that they want and the community relations program serves the company's marketing effort.

CHAPTER

7

7

Affirmative
Action Programs

As an entrepreneur dealing with people of many minority and ethnic groups, both sexes, the handicapped and all ages, your compliance with the affirmative action program may be required by law.

However, affirmative action is more than just something you may have to observe in order to stay on the right side of the law. It is also good business and, consequently, *good public relations.* Believe me, that is not just a one-liner or catchword created by the liberal establishment to further the civil rights cause. It is an honest-to-goodness fact which can be supported by case histories. In fact, the directors of the National Association of Manufacturers voted in May 1985 to adopt a statement backing affirmative action as "good business policy."

There is ample evidence that most American corporations, if given a choice, would retain affirmative action programs because of their public relations value, idealism on the part of top executives, the availability of more talent and the effect the elimination of the program would have on employee morale.

What makes the NAM action and the corporate position especially significant is the lack of support from the Reagan administration for some aspects of the affirmative action program. The administration feels that companies can reach a condition of true fairness in employment standards only by completely ignoring race and sex, not by choosing women and minorities over white men who apply for jobs. In mid-August 1985, the administration even proposed a presidential executive order which could end mandatory goals and timetables in affirmative action programs.

Yet, despite the absence of government support, companies have continued voluntarily with business as usual regarding affirmative action. Wouldn't you say that's a strong indication that affirmative action is good business — and good public relations?

Title VII of the Civil Rights Act of 1964 prohibits discrimination in employment. It specifies that an employer cannot consider race or sex in hiring decisions. Affirmative action, Title IX of the act, involves the implementation of an active outreach program to hire minorities and women with mandatory goals and time-tables. It goes beyond merely calling for an end to discrimination.

Regulations stemming from a 1965 executive order affect 115,000 private businesses that employ an estimated 23 million workers. Any company with a government construction contract of $10,000 or more must have affirmative action goals. Companies with federal contracts worth at least $50,000 must submit a written program to the Labor Department. Contact the Office of Federal Contract Compliance, Boston, Mass., if you have questions about your company's legal obligation for affirmative action goals.

NEGATIVE ACTION?

There are several forms of discrimination in the

business world. As an entrepreneur, company president and public relations officer, you should be aware of them and be prepared to explain them.

The gap between the median family income of black Americans and white Americans is enormous and results directly from this problem, which has existed for generations. In 1980, black family units were living on a median income of $12,674. The corresponding figure for whites was $21,904. For years, the proportion has remained about the same. Because of this wage discrimination, whites and nonwhites with the same education, same field and of the same sex draw different incomes.

Another form, occupational discrimination, has driven blacks into lower paid positions.

Investment money flows into white education while it only trickles into black institutions of higher learning. Consequently, a lower quality of education has been available to the nonwhite population. And despite the fact that people of differing races have spent the same number of years in school, there has been a wide gap in their economic rewards.

In employment, discrimination has been more evident during poor economic conditions when nonwhites have been the last to be hired and the first to be fired. This is largely an effect of past discrimination heightened by seniority plans which otherwise have been fair, sensible and acceptable. The unemployment problem also has increased for black persons because of their nonunion status. Union members generally have been the first to be hired and the last to be fired. It cannot be denied that a measure of racial bias has affected the decisions of company officials responsible for hiring employees. Companies that are sincere about removing this racial bias from their hiring practices would do well to address themselves to this problem.

As a public relations person, you do not have an easy task in selling your affirmative action program. It may help to emphasize income differences between minorities and the people who have benefited from past discrimination. The trick is to identify this social debt and provide remedies that result in no unfair penalties and do not damage investment incentive.

Affirmative action is not meant to be a tool for punishment. The purpose is to encourage a fairer distribution of income and opportunity, to create the distribution that would exist today if society had been open and fairly competitive all along. But, to use an old adage, the problem should be handled with a velvet glove and not a mailed fist. Individuals who are not minorities should not be asked to sacrifice their positions to satisfy this debt.

As a first step in your affirmative action plan, you might recognize this debt and then state that you wish to use the resources of your company to provide accelerated opportunities to minorities who have been deprived of income in the past.

THE COURTS AND AFFIRMATIVE ACTION

Since the Civil Rights Act of 1964, a number of court decisions have had an effect on affirmative action. Two Supreme Court cases, *Regents of the University of California* v. *Bakke* and *United Steelworkers of America* v. *Weber* have drawn a great deal of interest.

In the Bakke case, the legality of the special minority admissions program at the University of California — Davis Medical School was at issue. The school had earmarked up to 16 seats in the first year class for minority students. On June 28, 1978, the Supreme Court decided by a 5–4 margin to uphold the decision of the California Supreme Court striking down the special minority admissions program. The court ordered Allen Bakke to be admitted to the medical school. However, the Supreme Court said, also by a 5–4 vote, that colleges and universities could use race as a factor in determining who should be admitted.

Reaction to the decision was mixed. Some regarded the decision as harmful to blacks and other minorities. They viewed the decision to admit Bakke with alarm, but favored the court's approval of the use of race as a factor in the admissions process. Others praised the elimination of the school's minority admissions program, applauded the court for removing the special minority admissions plan, but disagreed with the use of race as a determining factor in admissions.

The Weber case dealt with the legality of a Kaiser Aluminum — United Steelworkers training program in which openings were based on a 50–50 ratio for blacks and whites. By a 5–2 vote, the court decided on June 29, 1979, to reverse the decisions of a Louisiana district court and the Fifth Circuit Court of Appeals and to support the program which reserved half of the training slots for blacks. This decision was criticized by conservative opponents of affirmative action and hailed by black leaders. The Weber decision was viewed as a victory for supporters of affirmative action in employment.

Other significant developments also have occurred recently on the affirmative action front. On June 13, 1984, the Supreme Court ruled that "seniority is more important than affirmative action goals when layoffs take place . . ." The case involved the layoffs of seventy-two whites in 1981 when the Memphis, Tennessee Fire Department was required to meet budget cuts and uphold affirmative action percentages at the same time. The people eventually were rehired, but the case went to the Supreme Court for a ruling.

Although the National Self-Monitoring Reporting System, an experimental program designed to ease the evaluation process for the government, has been in operation since November 1982, it was made known only in 1984. Initiated by AT&T and later including IBM, GM and Hewlett-Packard, the program allowed these firms to self-police their compliance with the Civil Rights Act. Women's groups and minorities challenged the Labor Department's attempt to expand the program in 1984 to include other large companies. They believed these firms could not evaluate their own actions without some bias.

The ever present equal-pay-for-equal-work controversy was extended to include the battle over "comparable worth." This concept questions the value of an individual to a firm or establishment, posing the question, "Are American women systematically and illegally underpaid for work that is different from but just as demanding as that done by men?" The issue of comparable worth could have serious ramifications to industry as well as all levels of government. On the basis of a study of employment discrimination and comparable worth by N. D. Willis and Associates, the state of Washington, was ordered by the U.S. District Court to give wage increases and four years of back pay to 15,000 workers, 90 percent of whom were women.

On August 24, 1984, President Reagan signed the Pension Law to Aid Women. The provisions include lowering the eligibility age for pension plan participation, permitting women on maternity leave (up to five years) to retain certain pension benefits and making it easier for a widow to get a share of her husband's pension.

CASE HISTORIES

Anne Fisher (1985) cites some examples of company executives who feel affirmative action is good for business.

"We will continue goals and timetables no matter what the government does," said John L. Hulck, chairman or Merck. "They are part of our culture and corporate procedures." John M. Stafford, president and chief executive officer of Pillsbury, adds, "It has become clear to us that an aggressive affirmative action program makes a lot of sense. So if the executive order is issued, it wouldn't affect us."

A survey conducted in late 1984 by Organization Resources Counselors, a New York-based consulting firm, also indicates the strong corporate commitment to affirmative action. Over 90 percent of the chief executive officers of large corporations reported that their companies established numerical objectives to achieve corporate objectives that did not pertain to government regulations. And of 128 who responded, 122 chief executive officers said they would continue to use numerical objectives to measure the progress of women and minorities in their corporations, regardless of government requirements.

Those who are opposed to affirmative action sometimes assert that goals and timetables are tantamount to quotas. However, corporate America does not appear to share that belief. A 1983 Ford Foundation survey of forty-nine government contractors showed that they do not consider goals and timetables to be quotas. In fact, they were opposed to quotas on the basis of race or sex. Even the NAM policy statement, which described affirmative action as good business, did not define goals as quotas. "Goals, not quotas, are the standards to be followed in the implementation of such programs," the statement specified.

William S. McEwen, director of equal opportunity affairs at Monsanto and chairman of NAM's human resources committee, told a congressional subcommittee recently that NAM is in favor of affirmative action, but not of quotas. "Business," he said, "sets goals and timetables for every aspect of its operation — profits, capital investment, productivity increases. Setting goals for minority and female participation is simply a way of measuring progress."

There probably are several reasons why companies are wedded to their affirmative action programs, not the least of which is their public relations value. Idealism on the part of top executives is one factor which cannot be ruled out. Another is expansion of the talent pool, which boosts productivity. When a company already has a firmly entrenched affirmative action plan in operation, the elimination of that program would result in complaints and seriously affect the morale of female and minority employees.

Sylvia Gerst, manager of affirmative action at Hewlett-Packard, emphasized the value of affirmative action in the computer industry. She pointed out that the industry is expanding so fast that "there are more opportunities than people. Minorities and women are enhancing our R&D work force." Ms. Gerst described the company's Student Employment and Educational Development program, which trains more than 500 college students including many women, blacks and Hispanics, each summer in the participant's chosen fields. About 60 percent of these students end up working for Hewlett-Packard after they graduate from college. "We look at this as a strategic long-term effort to get good people," she said. "Whether or not goals and timetables continue to be required, we expect this to keep getting bigger."

Peggy Sieghardt, division manager of human resources at AT&T, also commented on the customer relations value of affirmative action. "Everyone is a potential customer of AT&T, and they look at us. Why would someone want to be a customer of an all-white company?"

Despite the fact that Avon has only one division that is a government contractor and is not required by law to have corporate goals and timetables, the firm has established an aggressive affirmative action program. The company sells 20 percent of its cosmetics to minorities and almost all of its sales are to women. Phillip Davis, who heads Avon's affirmative action program, notes that when the program was started, "the aim was to bring in victims of past discrimination. Now that minorities have come in the door, the job of affirmative action is to oversee the upward mobility of these people. That is the focus in the 1980's."

AFFIRMATIVE ACTION IS HERE TO STAY

So, whether or not the administration decides to put an end to mandatory goals and timetables, it appears that affirmative action is here to stay. Maybe that is the way it should be — private enterprise voluntarily continuing its affirmative action, not because it has to by law, but because it is morally right, good for business and *good public relations.*

THE HANDICAPPED

Minorities and women are not the only victims of discrimination. The mentally and physically handicapped, as well as the aged, also have suffered discrimination, sometimes accidental and well-meant and sometimes intentional.

William Kroger (1979) relates the case of Elizabeth Cleghorn, president and founder of Richmond Combined Enterprises, Inc., of Richmond, Indiana. Her firm, which manufactures wire harnesses for electronic products, hires fifty-two production employees. Fifty-two of them are handicapped.

Ms. Cleghorn describes them as "the best people on earth to hire. They take great pride in the quality of their work. Many of them feel that this is the first time they have had the opportunity to do quality work, and they also have a chance to be independent."

Employing the handicapped is not a new practice for the Bulova Watch Co., either. After World War II, the firm opened the Joseph Bulova School of Watchmaking in Woodside, New York to help returning disabled veterans. The inscription on the school's cornerstone reads, "To Serve Those Who Served Us." What could be better public relations than that?

The school has produced more than 1,400 graduates. Disabled civilians were enrolled in 1950. The school was financed entirely by private funding, much of it coming from the Bulova Watch Co.

Another company that has found that it's good business as well as good public relations to hire the handicapped is GPK Products, Inc., of Fargo, North Dakota, which manufactures plastic sewer fittings.

Donald S. Goering, general manager and part-owner of GPK, notes, "When we were growing, disabled people would apply for a job, and we would say 'why not?' We hire people who are handicapped and treat them as normal people."

About 15 percent of the work force at GPK is physically or mentally handicapped. Although they usually
require more training, Goering maintains that his disabled employees are good business. "Once they've gotten into the groove, they're very dependable," he said.
"That's worth a lot."

Hiring the disabled also helps nondisabled workers, Goering emphasizes, "It makes them appreciate
that they aren't handicapped; it makes them happier
with their own lives."

GPK Products was a finalist for the 1978 Small
Business Employer of the Year award presented by the
President's Committee on Employment of Handi-
capped. How's that for public relations?

SERVICE CLUBS

In addition to private business, service clubs also
are active in the movement to find gainful employment
for the handicapped. The Chicago Rotary Club has
worked for years with the Rehabilitation Institute of
Chicago, a private hospital, to help the disabled. After
rehabilitation, many handicapped persons could not
go back to their previous occupations. The Rotary Club
got involved in retraining them for new careers, and it
has helped many disabled persons find jobs since the
program began.

What's more, the effort to help the disabled has expanded to more than forty-five Rotary Clubs involving
over 2,500 businesses and professional persons repre-
senting different firms and opportunities. The Rota-
rians feel the disabled are preferable employees
because they have a lower absentee record and higher
dedication to performance and quality output. In fact,
in many cases they out-perform nondisabled people in
the same jobs.

Lions International also helps the disabled
through eye programs which began years ago. These
services include eye banks, screening examinations

and obtaining glasses. Some Lions Clubs also have established hearing programs.

HISTORY OF HANDICAPPED

Before the 1970s, the handicapped person had little chance of living a normal life. Most people had a paternal attitude toward the disabled. They thought of them in terms of wheelchair, cane, sign language or braille. Yet, persons suffering from heart disease, emphysema, arthritis and other ills, including alcoholism, now are classified as disabled. Businesses were reluctant to employ someone whose eyesight was impaired, hearing was inadequate or mobility was limited. The fact that many handicapped persons received little or no formal education was another factor in their failure to enter the work force. However, the business community now is becoming aware of the value of hiring the disabled both in terms of quality work and public relations.

The movement to hire the handicapped has been aided by the enactment of such legislation as the Education for All Handicapped Children Act in the early 1970s and the Rehabilitation Act in 1973.

THE OVER-THE-HILL SYNDROME

As head of your company, don't let yourself get locked into the syndrome of labeling a worker as "over the hill" because of advancing years. That kind of thinking went out with the hysteria of the 1960s when everyone over thirty was considered to have one foot in the grave.

Age discrimination is against the law these days, of course, but even if it were not, you would be foolish indeed to refuse a job to a candidate or to put one of your employees out to pasture who is in his fifties or sixties.

There is nothing worse than wasting a mind, whether the individual is young, black or Hispanic, a handicapped person, a woman or an aged person.

You've got to strike a good balance in your work force, especially if your business involves frequent contact with the public. If your customers and business associates represent all age groups, your employees also should be at all age levels. The older ones may not be able to spit out the answers with the rapidity of an automatic weapon, but what they lack in this type of firepower will be more than tempered by an ability which comes only with experience and maturity.

HISTORY OF AFFIRMATIVE ACTION

In the implementation of the affirmative action program, entrepreneurs have been plagued with problems that sometimes defy solution related to minorities, age and sex. Often these problems degenerate into a confrontation between the community and civil rights activists. Sometimes the issues are embedded in a quagmire of litigation or governmental regulatory action.

Richard F. America (1983) contends this syndrome can be linked to a failure of public relations or public affairs strategies based on an inadequate understanding of the economic history of race relations in this country. He feels that PR staffs that serve chief executives and strategic planners need to understand the benefits to the whole community as well as the cost to minorities of past discrimination.

Companies have adopted policy statements on equal opportunity and affirmative action, but few have explained why they have these policies beyond an expression of belief in equal opportunity.

America cites the case of Dean Witter Reynolds, which entered a preliminary agreement in February 1982 to pay $4.5 million over a period of five years to settle a sex and race discrimination class-action suit. The terms of the agreement provided $1.8 million to 4,000 female black and Hispanic employees and persons who applied for jobs from 1978 through 1981. The agreement earmarked $2.9 million for affirmative action recruiting and hiring.

However, Dean Witter admitted no discrimination or violation of federal law in the settlement, a common legal practice in such cases.

America believes that cases settled in this manner without explanation create problems such as the lack of justice and the relative disadvantage encountered by white persons who apply to Dean Witter. He feels that PR professionals should work with management in finding answers to the following questions:

1. Does the company have a racial problem in employment?
2. What is the problem?
3. Did the company contribute to it historically?
4. If the company did not, does it have any current affirmative obligation?
5. If it feels that it does, what is it?
6. Is it redistributive? From whom to whom?
7. Can the company manage it without undue consequences to morale and productivity?
8. What is the law?
9. Is the company in compliance?
10. If not, what should it do to comply?

America emphasizes that one of the points public relations practitioners have failed to drive home is the fact that middle, upper-middle, and upper income whites have been the recipients of earnings which have been diverted from blacks for more than fifteen generations because of racial prejudice. This money has been denied blacks in labor and capital markets until recently. Earnings that would have gone to blacks in a free market went to whites instead. The nonblack population got the jobs, training, loans, licenses, franchises, grants and other economic benefits, which were passed on from generation to generation.

Although some of us are civil rights activists and some are not, most of us believe this was wrong. This is why an effective public relations program should reflect this truth. Rather than simply stating your company's policies, your equal opportunity and affirmative action plan should specify who currently receives benefits wrongfully, rather than focusing exclusively on who bore the costs of exclusion from opportunity and economic participation. Dwelling on the cost is likely to affect public and employee opinion adversely, to lower morale and efficiency and, eventually, to spawn bitterness, resentment and accusations of "reverse discrimination."

Affirmative action programs that explain this racial economic history and profess a sincere effort to rectify a wrong situation appear to be more successful than those which refuse to admit that such a process of wrongful distribution of benefits has occurred. This approach is necessary in order to achieve interracial teamwork and accord, and, consequently, high performance and productivity in companies.

Clarence Thomas, chairman of the Equal Employment Opportunity Commission, also emphasized the need for a strong public relations thrust in the execution of affirmative action, adding

> We can never underestimate the importance of the power of reason or our responsibility to reason before getting involved in a federal case . . .
>
> We will attempt to create a climate which encourages public support and sensitivity toward civil rights issues. We will also attempt to act as a catalyst for encouraging constructive debate and creative questioning which will generate better ways to achieve equal employment opportunity for all Americans.
>
> It is high time that someone started to articulate the fundamental principles which we all share, the principles which unite everyone in this administration and the overwhelming majority of the American people in the area of civil rights. One of the essential functions of the federal government is to ensure that the civil rights of all Americans be protected. This is not an issue which can be compromised, and it is not an obligation which the federal government can shirk.

Thomas pointed out that "no one is his right mind seriously questions the legal and moral bankruptcy of discrimination." However, he notes "the same unanimity of opinion does not exist for affirmative action," which "has been and will continue to be a subject of hot debate because mere mention of the term divides interest groups into two warring camps: one hotly in favor and one hotly opposed."

The EEOC chairman charges that these

warring camps . . . . lose sight of the nature and purpose of equal employment opportunity laws. They lose sight of the fact that almost 30 percent of the minority families rely on incomes below the poverty level and the black teenage employment is near 50 percent. They lose sight of the fact that women, although heads of households in increasing numbers, earn only about 60 cents for each dollar that men earn. They lose sight of the fact that in this country 3.5 million persons of Spanish origin live below the poverty level. They lose sight of the fact that the chairman of the EEOC spent 17 years of his life (one-half) under strict segregation.

Thomas feels the "combatants" fail to pay significant attention to the

less dramatic, but ultimately more important, issues of devising more effective remedies which respond to the changing nature of discrimination. All of these unfortunate consequences flow from the nature of the debate over affirmative action. Even worse, this divisive debate results in general confusion and misunderstanding about affirmative action which, in turn, tends to undermine the effectiveness and legitimacy of the enforcement of civil rights laws. . . . We must attempt to bring out and clarify the issues obscured by this debate.

That is where you come in, Ms. company president.

Thomas goes on to define affirmative action as "the recognition that it is a further remedy designed to place a class, not specific victims of past discrimination, in the place where it theoretically would have been but for discrimination." Within that frame of reference, affirmative action could be used to describe any of your recruitment efforts designed to advance a class. It would not necessarily have to be successful. However, recruitment by itself, or the end of unlawful employment practices, is not considered to be affirmative action.

As the PR practitioner for your company, you should take special pains to interpret correctly any opposition to your affirmative action program. Such objections may not necessarily stem from insensitivity toward discrimination or civil rights issues. The antagonists may be expressing opposition to the method of affirmative action, not the ultimate goal of elevating a class to its rightful level of economic health. Affirmative action programs are not beyond question. However, in this particular case, it may be a matter of the end justifying the means.

GOOD PUBLIC RELATIONS

It bears repeating: there is nothing worse than wasting a mind. But, for the moment, let's shelve the moral aspects and look at the facts with the calculating mind of a businessperson. You can't afford to ignore affirmative action. In case after case, despite the lack of governmental support, American companies have continued their affirmative action programs. Why? Because it is good business and *good public relations*.

CHAPTER

8

8

Speaking Engagements

Your hands are cold and clammy. Your knees are shaking. Your mouth is dry. Your teeth are chattering. You are sure your fly is open. You have to live up to that glowing introduction from the master of ceremonies. You have to satisfy all those expectant faces in front of you. And you have to do it despite your sudden mental block. A nervous sigh escapes your lips and the ensuing breeze lifts one of your cue cards from the lectern. The card, experiencing the freedom of flight for the first time, flutters like a butterfly to the floor.

Join the club. We've all been there at one time or another. But cheer up, your fear of speaking before groups will not last forever. As you gain experience in the art of public speaking and follow a few simple rules of preparation and delivery, your anxiety will slowly disappear.

Direct person-to-person contact is one of the best ways of projecting a favorable image of your company, but it is impossible to speak personally to every individual who should receive your company's message.

The next best thing is talking to large numbers of persons.

BE SELECTIVE

If your time is limited, be selective about the groups you choose for your talks. Try to confine your audiences to groups in your company's immediate sphere of influence. These would include employees, customers, people living in the vicinity of your plant, stockholders and suppliers. Employees are particularly important because they are the ones who carry your company's message to the community in person-to-person contact. They can make or break your firm. Of course, you can't really refuse the request of the local Boy Scout troop either. It's not good community relations. They are the leaders of tomorrow, and their parents may be the leaders and customers of today.

But, if you have an opportunity to pick and choose, the Chamber of Commerce is a good organization for the type of people you want to reach. Other good groups to have on your speaking schedule are the Rotary, Kiwanis and Lions Clubs, the American Legion and Veterans of Foreign Wars, the Masons, Knights of Columbus and B'nai B'rith. Don't forget manufacturers' asssociations either.

CHOOSING YOUR COMPANY SPEAKER

Be honest with yourself. You may be a whiz kid in the brains department and great at managing people in your company, but if you are a weak, timid and bashful speaker, you shouldn't be the one to represent your company at the lectern. In fact, you could make an exciting message sound like you are reading an obituary.

Look around your company. One of your vice presidents may be the ideal person to reflect that air of confidence, vigor, strength and expertise so necessary to give the right impression of your company. But, if you are the owner of a small firm and you are the only person available, you will have to brush up on speaking skills yourself.

KNOW YOUR AUDIENCE

One of the first steps in the preparation of your speech is to determine the make-up of the audience. Tailor the talk to your listeners. The engineering society wouldn't be very interested in a presentation on the care and feeding of the Eurasian squirrel monkey. Save that one for the zookeepers' association.

Know the purpose of your talk. Is it informative, educational, pure entertainment, an attempt to raise funds or are you beating the drums for a cause? Then decide on one subject and do your homework. Thoroughly research your topic, especially if the crowd is familiar with it.

THE FORMAT

Before you prepare your speech, you should decide the format. Do you want to use file cards with notes, an outline or a full speech? Many speakers like to write out their talk, word for word. The problem with this method is that the speaker has a tendency to read directly from the manuscript to the audience. The delivery becomes stiff, unspontaneous and boring. The speaker who reads the speech from a paper also loses eye contact with the audience, which is an essential part of delivery. A speech should sound more like a casual conversation with the audience rather than like formal writing.

The off-the-cuff speaker who steps up to the lectern and begins to talk without research or advance preparation is another thing. This is fine as far as the spontaneity factor is concerned. However, very few people can get away with it. If the topic is simple, you may achieve some success with this method, but with more complex subjects, you must be completely knowledgeable about your topic to be able to pull facts off the top of your head.

A happy medium is to record the results of extensive research in an outline (or on 3 by 5-inch index cards) of the main points. Use these points as cues to content and sequence.

WRITING THE SPEECH

As you prepare your speech, you might give special attention to five points:

1. Credibility
2. Commitment
3. Organization
4. Conciseness
5. Practice

You can achieve credibility through experience, proper research and adequate knowledge of the subject. You will have trouble holding the attention of the audience if these ingredients are missing.

If you are not committed to a subject or if it is not important to you, forget about the talk. An audience can easily sense that you are bored with your own presentation and they will react in a similar manner.

To achieve good organization, your talk must have an effective format. And you should choose the format that best suits your style whether it be a manuscript, outline or index cards.

A concise talk will hold the attention of listeners. If you go far afield with superfluous language, excessive quotations and examples, you will quickly lose the audience.

The more you practice in advance, the more effective your speech will be in front of a live audience. Cover the main points so it flows easily from the lectern to your listeners. You don't have to memorize your speech. In fact, learning the speech word for word might even work against you because it could result in the loss of the spontaneity factor.

If you decide to write out your speech word for word, the first rule to remember is to make the talk sound like it wasn't written out. That sounds like a lot of double talk, doesn't it?

Above all, be sensitive to the difference between a written message and an oral one. An oral message need not have the same readability factors as one that is written. A written report usually has the wrong structure for effective oral presentation because it contains too much and the emphasis is wrong. Some speech writers use a term they call the "bell curve" to describe the structure of a talk. Visualize a bell standing upright and trace its outline. The line starts at a low point, rises to a high curve or apex and returns to a low point. In like manner, you begin your speech on a low key, rise to a climax in the middle of it and return to a low key.

An apt guideline for speechwriting is the "rule of three"

1. Tell them what you're going to tell them
2. Tell them
3. Tell them what you told them

Before you write the speech, decide its length and stay within the time restraints. I have seen some excellent orators destroy their own work by rambling on and on in a speech, not knowing when to stop. Ask how much time has been allotted to your talk. Then figure five to eight double-spaced pages of text for every ten minutes of speaking. An ideal pace for your talk is 120–180 words per minute.

Know the jargon of your audience and write your speech accordingly. Use short sentences and direct language. Speak directly to your audience, using such words as "you" and "we."

Quotations add to a speech, but don't overuse them. Your manuscript should be written in full capital letters so you can pick up the words at a glance. And the sentences should be double-spaced. If it would make it easier to read quickly, you could even triple-space the manuscript.

Rehearse your speech with a friend before the actual presentation. The gestures you make in your talk are very important. Mark key words on the manuscript so they will stand out and you can spot them quickly. You could underline a word or phrase you wish to emphasize. Use a wavy line to remind you to undulate a hand, make arrows pointing up or down to indicate a rise or fall in volume, and an asterisk to signal a fist pound on the lectern, a foot stomp or a shout. It doesn't matter what symbols you use as long as you can understand them.

However, in all cases, your talk should appear to be spontaneous, even though it isn't.

Speakers generally begin a speech with small talk or a joke. But, if you will accept a word of caution, be careful with the humor. If you are speaking to the funeral directors or the state organization to aid the mentally retarded, your attempt at humor in these areas may backfire. You could leave a bad taste in the mouths of your listeners that would color their reaction to your entire speech and nullify whatever points you are trying to make. Remember the time President Lyndon Johnson lifted his beagles by their ears? That may have been funny to some people but it also invoked the wrath of many others.

Establish a rapport with your audience. A favorite trick with seasoned speakers is to pick a character from the audience and proceed in the following manner, "Oh, I see we have Joe Dokes with us tonight. Joe and I go back a long way. I can remember when Joe and I used to work together on the garbage scow. We used to feed the sea gulls on our lunch break. One day Joe got too close to the edge and fell . . ."

After the introduction, you come to the body of the speech. Don't try to make too many points. Unlike the reader, the listener is unable to turn pages and review sections if the message is not clear. For that reason, you should repeat your point often. Two points is the maximum number you should attempt to make in a 10 to 15-minute speech. You can make three or four in an hour-long talk.

Repeat your points over and over again. The audience may miss them the first time. And support your points with plenty of examples. The end of your talk should contain a conclusion and a summary or recommendations.

Don't try to impress your audience with twenty-dollar words when you can express your meaning just as well with a ten-center. You won't fool anyone. Audiences appreciate simple, direct language so you will establish more rapport.

Read the speech to yourself at least five times and make sure you know how to pronounce all the words. By reading it to yourself, you will unconsciously memorize enough of it that you will not be chained to the manuscript when you present your speech before others.

If you are writing out the full text of your speech, do not split up a paragraph from one page to another. No one wants to wait for a speaker to turn the page to hear the end of a sentence. Indent the first line of all paragraphs and keep them short, no more than ten lines long. Number the pages just in case you drop them at the podium.

Don't try to write a speech that will consume your full time allotment. Save a couple of minutes in case you want to ad lib or answer questions.

LITTLE DETAILS

Do some advance preparation at the setting of your talk. If everything is right, you will be relaxed when you make your speech and do a better job. Consequently, the audience will relax and be better listeners.

Request a lectern on which to place your manuscript, outline or index cards. It will give you a place to set your papers and shield them so they won't be so obvious to the audience. Don't staple or clip your manuscript together. As you read or refer to your manuscript, slide the completed pages across the lectern so that no one sees when you have finished one page and started another. It is less distracting than lifting up each page and putting it down.

Make sure the lighting is good so you won't have to squint at the pages. If you have an opportunity, check the public address system before your talk. There is nothing worse than a PA system that squeaks, squawks, hums and bellows. It can completely ruin your talk.

I can remember one function where former Congressman David Emery was scheduled to speak. When he stepped up to the microphone, the system was completely dead. Fortunately, the U.S. representative was an electrical engineer before he entered political life. He calmly disassembled the microphone and repaired it as the audience waited patiently. Emery then delivered his talk. It even added a little levity to the occasion.

If you plan to illustrate your talk with slides, make sure your projector is in good working order. And know how to use it.

APPEARANCE

In this day and age when anything goes in some circles, it is difficult to give advice about personal appearance. When in doubt on the proper attire for a speaking engagement, I suggest you exercise a bit of common sense. Use the old adage, "When in Rome, do as the Romans do." If you've been asked to speak to the Chamber of Commerce, Rotary Club, engineers or other such groups as president of your company, a business suit is definitely in order. On the other hand, such formal dress might turn people off at meetings of artists or writers.

But whatever you decide to wear, you should always be neat and clean.

THE DELIVERY

Believe it or not, your method of presenting a speech will have much more impact on an audience than what you actually say. Take the veteran politician.

He can speak for more than an hour to an enthralled audience and say virtually nothing. Through long experience, he has acquired, either consciously or unconsciously, the ability to hold the attention of his listeners through gestures and intonations.

Every speaker has his or her own personal style. But certain basic actions are essential in the delivery of all good talks. Delivery is nothing more than the manner in which you speak to your audience. In fact, it is only doing what comes naturally. If you were relating a funny story or a choice bit of gossip to an old friend, you wouldn't stand like a mechanical dummy, speak in a deadly monotone, gabble inarticulately or stare at your shoes. You would look your friend in the eye, change your facial expressions, wave your arms, pound your fist in your palm or stomp your foot on the floor for emphasis. Your voice would rise from a whisper to a shout. Your tone would vary. You might pause for a reaction from your friend. You might shift your body position, even walking from one end of the room to the other.

Yet, for reasons beyond the scope of this book, many persons freeze when they are about to speak to large groups of people. And listeners, sensing nervousness in the speaker, react in like manner. They become uncomfortable, begin to shift in their seats, cough and whisper. They can't wait for the talk to be over. They may even walk out, slamming doors in the process. However, American speakers are much more fortunate than their European counterparts. At least their audiences are polite. In some foreign countries, no speech is considered complete without its hecklers.

If you want to hold the attention of your audience, work on your delivery techniques. Slow the pace of your talk. A good speed is 120–180 words per minute. If you reach a point in your speech when you think the audience should applaud, laugh or even ask a question, stop for a moment and let them get into the act. Such a pause also will give your audience a cue to respond to your talk.

Make sure you are speaking loudly enough for everyone in the room to hear. Don't be afraid to ask, "Can everybody in the back row hear me?" Adjust your voice to the size of the room. If you are speaking to a group in a small committee room, don't assault their ears with a great booming voice. On the other hand, don't whisper to an audience in a large hall. With modern electronics and public address systems, acoustics no longer pose a great problem to speakers in large areas, but you should know how to do without PA systems. The person in charge of arrangements may have forgotten this little item or there could be an equipment breakdown. And you may not be an electrical engineer.

Speak clearly to your audience. Do not slur your words. All the advance preparation in the world will mean nothing if your speech lacks clarity. When you rehearse your talk, you might ask a friend to check your enunciation.

Did you ever watch a police officer directing traffic at a busy intersection? If she has been doing it for a number of years, it is both entertaining and educational to watch her in action. She positions her body like a fine musical instrument, bending, leaning, swaying, crouching, pointing, waving and nodding. She may scowl at an inattentive driver, smile at a friend or make a funny face for a youngster. It is perfectly obvious what she wants a driver to do even though she has not said a word.

As a speaker, you can use your body, as well as your voice, in the same way. Give your audience something to watch. Facial expressions and intonations indicate emotion and attitudes. Emphasize a point with a vertical or horizontal wave of your hand. You can convey announcement by stepping back, arching your back and spreading your arms. For confidentiality, lean forward and bring your hands together. Make sure such gestures are apparent to everyone in the room. In large halls, your body language should be exaggerated; in smaller rooms it can be more subdued.

Above all, exude an air of confidence. If you act confident, you will feel confident and, consequently, earn the credibility of your audience.

Let your listeners know you care about them. Maintain constant eye contact. Shift from one person to the other. If they appear to be confused, give them more detail about your subject. If they seem to be bored or inattentive, change your mode of delivery. Move around the room or vary the tone of your voice.

Last, but not least, avoid the "ers," "uhs," "ahs," "you knows" and other meaningless sounds that you hear in some talks.

The more you speak, the more you will develop confidence in yourself. Be aware of your bad speaking habits, but don't dwell on them. As your podium time increases, they will slowly disappear.

GRAPHICS

Flip charts, overhead transparencies, posters, slides or films are helpful if you wish to clarify, reinforce, amplify, focus attention or emphasize points in your talk.

In addition, they give the speaker an opportunity to get his head together and slow down his speech. The pause also gives the audience a chance to absorb the points you have already made.

However, you might consider a word of caution. Keep your graphics simple. Remember, the audience gets little more than a glance at the visual material. Unless your listener has a photographic mind, a voluminous list of numbers or written material may serve only to confuse or disorient him.

If you have one or two points you wish to emphasize, you might display them on a poster or chart which could be on view throughout your talk. This would help to reinforce the points.

Photographs or slides which require a great deal of study to understand do not add much to your talk. If you want to show your audience a construction site, don't exhibit an aerial photo that would require a magnifying glass to decipher. Show them a close view of the site even if it does not cover the whole property.

Make sure your graphics are large enough for easy viewing by every person in the room. Another argument against the use of large lists of complicated numbers or written material is the fact that only persons in the front row can see them.

Sometimes you can reinforce your points by passing out samples of your product to every member of the audience. This is fine if your listeners don't become more interested in your product than your talk.

On one occasion, I was scheduled to give a presentation about a railroad entrepreneur. I started off my talk by winding up a toy train and running it across the floor. That may have been childish, but it served the purpose. The visual aid was simple. My audience was in good humor and thinking about trains. And I had their attention.

Working models also are very helpful in a talk, but they have their disadvantages. They can break down and fail to work right, distracting the audience and disrupting your talk.

One of the best visual aids is the overhead transparency. Its brightness holds the attention of the audience. You can add information, arrows, circles and underlines. You can also mask sections which might distract the audience.

Whatever form of graphics you choose for your presentation, you would do well to make sure in advance that all equipment is available and in good running order. Check the lectern area for needed electrical outlets.

SPEAKERS BUREAU

If you are the president of a moderate-sized company, you may want to consider establishing a speakers bureau. This is nothing more than a list of persons who are available to speak on a variety of subjects. You could have as few as ten or as many as 100 on your list.

There is no end to the number of different subjects that could be included in your speakers bureau. They could range from accounting, management techniques, design and present trends in industry, to the future of the business community and the possibility of private enterprise taking over governmental functions such as the operation of the prison systems.

If your company manufactures flangemeters for the Space Shuttle, you've got a built-in potential for audience interest in your operation.

However, you don't have to limit your speakers bureau list to business-oriented subjects. Your employees may have a number of hobbies and outside interests that would make excellent topics for public talks. Your vice president may be an amateur astronomer. Your company accountant may be able to provide tips on preparing income taxes.

These talks do not necessarily have to deal directly with the company or its business. Just the fact that you or your vice president are associated with the Colonial Gidget Co. is enough to enhance the image of your firm.

If you have a few bucks in your public relations budget, you may want to design a brochure to publicize your speakers bureau. You could have an attractive one prepared by a professional printer at a cost of less than $500. However, if you would rather spend your public relations allotment in other areas, a series of typewritten pages reproduced by your photocopier would serve the same purpose.

You don't have to be a graphic artist to design a useful and handsome speakers bureau brochure. The first step is to send a memo to all your company employees to generate interest in a speakers bureau. Above all, don't exclude any of your employees. Your company custodian may be an authority on growing mushrooms. Your cafeteria manager may be a graduate of the Culinary Institute of America and an expert on the culinary arts. Persons who can speak on the subject of food preparation are much in demand these days. If you don't believe it, check your local bookstore for the number of cookbooks on the racks, or newspapers and magazines for food-related stories. Even your electric bill is accompanied by a brochure containing recipes.

Don't forget the young people on your loading docks. Competitive and long distance running, pumping iron and physical fitness are popular subjects for both men and women.

Your speakers bureau memo should ask for the full names of the employees, their company positions, qualifying data such as education or experience, and their area(s) of expertise. If you are the president of a moderate-sized company and you have the time, you would get better results if you approached each employee individually. There is nothing like the personal touch and it would give your employees a warm feeling to be asked by the president himself to join the speakers bureau.

If your survey produces no more than twenty-five speakers, you could get away with an eight-page, 4 by 9-inch brochure, stapled in the center. The listing would fit into that size comfortably. If you have no more than ten persons on your list, a four-page publication probably would be sufficient.

The first page of your brochure should contain the name of your company, its location, your company logo and the words, "Speakers Bureau." Keep it simple. Don't try to make it into an advertising brochure by touting your company's product or service. You will accomplish more with the subtle approach. The fact that you are providing the public service of a speakers bureau will speak for itself as far as public relations is concerned.

The second page of your brochure should contain information about the policies of your speakers bureau. You might give general information about it including the fact that speakers will "share their expertise with service clubs, church and civic groups, schools and professional organizations or any group of persons desiring the services of a speaker."

Most speakers bureaus established for the purpose of public relations offer their speakers free of charge. However, any organization which customarily pays an honorarium for its speakers should extend the same courtesy to your personnel. Also, if your speakers have to go a great distance for the talk, the sponsoring organization should be willing to pick up travel expenses. The speaker should not have to pay for his own meal if it is a dinner or luncheon meeting.

Don't forget to recognize the employee who contributes to company public relations through the speakers bureau. Give him credit in the company newsletter or on the bulletin board. By all means, contact the media to see if they are interested in covering the talk. By now, you are familiar with the policies of your local newspaper. If you feel the talk has enough news value for publication, send the media an advance story about two weeks before the talk and a follow-up story as soon as possible after the program. Check with the sponsoring organization first to avoid duplication of publicity.

Your brochure also should specify the person to contact to make arrangements for a speaker, with a telephone number and a mailing address. The person should be contacted at least three weeks in advance of the date to give the speaker ample time to prepare the talk.

The next page of your brochure could contain a list of topics or titles of presentations in alphabetical order with the last name of the speaker beside them. The list of topics could be followed on succeeding pages by the full names of the speakers in alphabetical order, their titles or positions with the company, qualifications and subjects. Thus, the program chairman of a sponsoring organization could choose a speaker either by subject or by name.

Your speakers bureau brochure should be distributed widely throughout the region. Every organization that might desire a speaker should receive a copy. These could include service clubs, religious organizations, professional groups, schools, business-oriented organizations and social groups. You should be able to get a list of organizations in the area from your chamber of commerce. And, of course, the city directory and telephone book is helpful. You might also leave copies of your brochure at the city hall, a doctor's waiting room or any public place.

When you establish your speakers bureau, prepare a news release for the newspapers circulating in your area. Most newspapers are willing to run a story about a new speakers bureau with the speakers and subjects if the list is not too long.

You should update the speakers bureau brochure at least every two years to reflect any changes in the speakers or their subjects.

Your Resource List or List of Experts, already covered in Chapter 4, also may be included in your brochure at the end of the list of speakers. If you recall, the Resource List contains the names of persons in your company the media can call if they need an expert opinion on a subject.

There you are, Company President. You now have the skills for effective public speaking. Step up to the lectern. Your audience is waiting.

CHAPTER

9

9

Writing for Success

As an entrepreneur, you have nurtured an idea from inception, through development and, finally, to fruition. You now are the owner of a thriving firm which is expanding daily and making a significant impact on the business community. You have created new jobs, broadened the tax base, and contributed to the Gross National Product.

But you, more than anyone, know that didn't happen by accident. You put in long hours, burned the candle at both ends, talked to many people, did much studying and tried a lot of new things. Some succeeded and some failed.

Along the way, you have picked up a wealth of information. Your mind is a storehouse of data on research and development, manufacturing, marketing and public relations techniques.

So why not share your business expertise with others who may want to walk the same path as you? In other words, why not try your hand at writing?

"Wait a minute," you say. "I know my way around

the business world pretty well. I can spot a good investment or a phony operation a mile away. But writing? I can't even write a decent business letter without going through gyrations of mental anguish. Ask my high school English teacher. I couldn't write my way out of a paper bag with a sharp pencil."

Nothing worthwhile is easy, including writing, but, by establishing a successful business, you've already shown that you have the dedication, drive, ambition, determination, and entrepreneurial spirit it takes. Why not apply these same qualities to a writing career?

You won't be the first professional to embark on a second career. There is no profession more demanding than medicine. Yet, I could name a number of doctors, including Frank Slaughter and Benjamin Spock, who are successful authors. If I had a nickel for every lawyer who wrote a book, I could retire. There also are numerous businessmen like yourself who have entered the writing field. They include specialists in investments, economics, stocks, bonds, business consulting, marketing, computers, finance and interest rates.

Why should you do it? The reasons are not completely aesthetic or altruistic. The writer is the only professional who achieves true immortality, and there is nothing better than the deep satisfaction of seeing one's name on a magazine article or book. However, a more practical reason is the purpose for which this book was written. Can you think of a better device for public relations than having your name appear on an article or book as an authority on a business subject? That would establish your standing with your colleagues, other business associates, customers and the community as a whole. And there is nothing wrong with a little extra money when the royalties begin to roll in.

If company business demands too much of your time or if you feel that writing is not your thing, there is another way of getting your ideas into print. Hire a ghostwriter to pick your brains and put the result into literary form for a book or article. And you will get the credit for the work. A well-established writer will even help you find a publisher. Of course, your ideas must have enough merit to interest a publishing house.

I'm sure you have seen many books by celebrities on the market. Most likely, they were actually written by a ghostwriter. The usual method is to sign a contract with a publisher and then make a separate agreement with a writer to produce the book.

I know of one case where two auctioneers had an excellent idea for operating their business. However, they had neither the time nor the writing skills to prepare a book. They engaged a ghostwriter and, at this time, a potentially successful book is in the works.

Let's backtrack to the original idea of business writing. Before we take on a major project, flex your literary muscles a bit by trying some articles in trade journals, business magazines or company publications.

If you know a friend who has been successful in the writing field, why not ask for advice? You might even make some kind of financial arrangement and ask him or her to read your copy.

TRADE JOURNALS

Trade journals are magazines whose editorial content is designed only for persons in a specific trade or profession. There is at least one trade journal for every major profession ranging from advertising and lumbering to water supply and sewage disposal. There are also general business magazines which often are interested in articles on investment and finance or stories with a regional angle.

COMPANY PUBLICATIONS

Sponsored publications, also known as house magazines, house organs or company publications, are magazines produced by business firms, institutions, associations, unions or specialty publishers. They usually are given away to employees, customers or friends of the organization.

There are two types of company publications. The internal publication is written for employees, dealers and salespeople of a company. The external goes either to stockholders or the general public to give a good impression of the company. It also may be sent to persons who are influential in using the company's product or service.

Company publications are excellent, well-paying markets for writers of all levels of experience. For example, *Exxon U.S.A. Magazine* pays $1,000 to $1,500 for articles from 2,000 to 2,500 words on such subjects as the firm's public affairs interests and concerns in the United States, environmental conservation, business economics and public energy policy. *Raytheon Magazine* pays $750 to $1,250 for articles ranging from 800 to 1,200 words.

TYPES OF ARTICLES

There are two types of articles you may want to consider as you take the first step in your new writing career. The how-to-do-it piece should be written in simple, easy-to-understand language about some process or technique you have found to be successful in your business. The success article describes how a particular businessperson made money and excelled through various techniques or adherence to certain principles. If you feel that is a fair description of your own operation, the success story may be an ideal subject for your first article.

SELECTING AN ARTICLE

As a successful entrepreneur, you have already proven yourself in the idea department. Choosing a topic for your magazine article is only an extension of your expertise in this area. Jot down some of the systems or techniques that have contributed to the successful development of your company. Can you attribute your firm's rise to management, accounting procedure, purchasing, investment, employment policy, marketing or manufacturing processes? Or, maybe you have developed a new wrinkle in public relations that would make a good article.

Your idea should be fresh, innovative and as specific as possible. A story about business in general stands little chance with trade journals, business magazines and company publications.

Your next stop should be at the library. If possible, choose a library in a good-sized city or university so you will have a wide choice of material. Use the *Reader's Guide to Periodical Literature*, the *Business Periodical Index* and the *Index to the Wall Street Journal* to check for previous articles on the subject you have chosen. Librarians can be very helpful if you have problems. If your subject has been covered thoroughly within the last five years, you would do well to choose another.

CHOOSING A MAGAZINE

When you have decided on a subject, your next step is to select a publication. *Writer's Market* or the *Ayer Directory of Publications* are excellent sources of information about publications that might be interested in your article. When you find such a magazine, return to the library and check several recent issues to determine their style and if they use the type of article you have in mind. If they do, you're in business. If your library doesn't have copies of the magazine you have selected, you might write to the magazine for a sample copy and their writer's guidelines.

THE QUERY LETTER

Now you are ready to approach the magazine you have selected for your article. Don't telephone the magazine: most magazine editors, and book editors for that matter, require an instrument called the "query letter."

A query letter is nothing more than a letter asking an editor if he would be interested in using your proposed story.

But, don't take the query letter lightly. It is very important, especially for a writer trying to sell a first article. If the query letter is poorly written, the editor will naturally assume that the article would be of the same quality, and your query letter most likely would be answered with a form letter along the lines of, "Your proposed article does not suit the needs of *The Entrepreneur* at this time. We wish you luck in marketing your article."

Most editors want query letters because their publications have specialized requirements. If a writer queries with a fresh idea for a piece, an editor may suggest a slant or focus that would make the article more appropriate for his readers.

WRITING THE QUERY LETTER

Some freelancers like to start a query letter in a cute manner with a question, a provocative statement or a paragraph which eventually will be the first paragraph of the article. I prefer to hit the nail directly on the head with a simple statement of what I want. My theory is that an editor who has just spent most of the day wading through an avalanche of cute query letters or who is nursing a cup of morning coffee in an attempt to return to the land of the living would appreciate a simple direct letter which gets right to the point.

Whatever type of introduction you choose, you should limit your letter to one single-spaced page. Sum up the major points of your article in no more than two paragraphs. If it takes you more than two paragraphs to hit the major points, you might reconsider the scope of the subject you have chosen. The article could be too complex and you should be more selective about pinning down a specific point of view you want to get across. However, make sure you do enough selling in the letter to persuade the editor to take a look at the article.

You should also be selective about your own qualifications for writing the article. You might mention
that you are president of the Colonial Gidget Co. If you
have a special background in the subject you have chosen, that should go into the letter. And if you have sold
previous articles to comparable magazines that the editor would respect, mention them, by all means. If not,
you don't have to mention that this is your first attempt
to market an article.

If the editor is interested in your suggestion, she
might reply that she would be glad to read it on speculation. That means she is interested enough to read your
manuscript, but has not committed herself to a promise
to buy it. Always enclose a self-addressed stamped envelope with your query letter or manuscript.

If you get a go-ahead from the editor, return an immediate answer. Tell him when he can expect the article
and make sure he receives it by that deadline or before.
If the editor isn't interested in your idea, try another
editor. You might emphasize a different angle in your
letter to the next editor. Study the list of magazine requirements in your directory and repeat the process.

Even if the editor asks to see your manuscript, you
may still get a rejection slip. If so, join the club. You
won't be a full-fledged writer until your house is wall-
papered with rejection slips. One of the problems in
writing is that editors rarely give criticism, construc-
tive or otherwise. But, who said writing was easy? You
might ask your writer friend for an opinion. Or, if you
really get desperate, you might approach your high
school English teacher.

But, remember one thing. If you had enough per-
sistence in your character to build a successful business, you certainly have enough to roll up your sleeves
and stick another piece of paper in your typewriter.

WRITING THE ARTICLE

Like the news release, the lead in a magazine article

is the most important part of the story. However, unlike the news release, the lead does not have to sum up the article or contain the who, what, where, when, why and how. The magazine lead is similar to the one in a feature story. It has a more literary style.

The lead should attract the attention of the reader. You can start with a quote, a question, an anecdote, a statement of fact or just a mood paragraph. The lead makes a person want to read the article.

Although you don't have to recapitulate the story, your lead should reflect the nature of the article. For example, you shouldn't put a sex lead on a story about long-term business investments just to grab the attention of the reader. A good article has a theme and a point of view and the ending should sum up and reinforce that point.

Before you begin your article, you should make a decision about the viewpoint. If the story is about your own company, product or service, you might use the first person, eye-witness viewpoint. That is the easiest viewpoint for the new writer and it strengthens the article's believability (I was there and I saw it myself). If your article is about another business, you should use the third person viewpoint. A writer must be directly involved in the story to use the first person.

Whatever viewpoint you decide, you should be consistent and carry it through the entire article. A single point of view provides unity to your article. If an article contains two points of view, devices must be used to achieve unity. As you gain expertise at writing, you will become adept at using such devices.

Thoroughly research your article before you begin to write, and check all facts carefully. Keep the dictionary constantly by your side. If you are not absolutely sure how a word is spelled, use it. The dictionary of a good writer should have that dog-eared look.

When you make a point in your article, illustrate that point with an example. Whenever possible, use quotations. They have a tendency to draw the reader into the article. The reader is able to identify with the person who is being quoted. He feels he is speaking directly to that person.

Before you mail the article to the magazine, edit your copy ruthlessly. Remove all extraneous material that does not support the theme of the article. Always polish and repolish your story.

THE BOOK MARKET

Fortunately, you have selected an excellent period in the publishing industry to try your hand at business writing. Today's book market, like the magazine market, is predominantly a nonfiction market.

Sure, you read about authors like Norman Mailer who are paid close to a million dollars for a single work of fiction. But for every author who makes it big in the fiction market, there are hundreds who are barely able to eke out a living. Writing fiction may be more romantic, but romance won't pay the mortgage, the car payment or the electric bill. If you want to see your work in print, the odds are better in the nonfiction market, especially for beginning writers.

The procedure for marketing a book varies from publisher to publisher. Some want a query letter first. Others ask for a query letter, synopsis, outline and sample chapters. Still others will accept the full manuscript immediately. Some will not consider an unsolicited manuscript under any circumstances. The requirements of each book publisher are listed in *Writer's Market* along with other such useful information as royalty policies, schedules and procedures, advances, number of titles published in the previous year, types of books, length and photography policies.

To market your book on business, I recommend that you proceed in the following manner. Find a publisher in the *Writer's Market* who is interested in the type of book you have in mind. Examine a copy of that publisher's current catalog for your kind of book. You can obtain copies of catalogs at most libraries and large bookstores, or you can get one by simply writing to the publisher and asking for a current catalog.

Get the titles of some of the publisher's recent books and see if you can find them in a bookstore or library. I am a great bookstore browser myself and have spent a good many hours pawing over the shelves without buying a book. (I have never been thrown out of a bookstore, though I probably have come close.) If you can locate some of the books, skim them for style and other information that will be useful to you in writing your book.

Now you are ready for action. Follow the publisher's instructions in the *Writer's Market*. Your query letter should be similar to the one for magazine articles. If the publisher wants an outline, write a synopsis and a paragraph for each chapter. If the firm also wants sample chapters, you will have to get to work. If you send a completed manuscript that does not meet the firm's needs, you will get an automatic rejection. However, if you send an outline, an editor may make a few revisions to meet the firm's needs and you will be in business. If you can stand more repetition at this point, I would like to reemphasize that you should send a self-addressed stamped envelope with everything you mail to a publisher.

Don't hold your breath while you wait for a reply from a publisher. The best you can expect is a month from the time you have mailed your material. You are fortunate if you get a decision within six weeks after mailing. Seven weeks is average and three months is not unusual. After that you should send another query letter. I once waited two years before getting an answer from a publisher. But that is an extreme case.

At any rate, if you receive a contract in the mail, it will make it all worthwhile. When you finish celebrating, you should examine the contract. If you are a beginning writer, you are in a tough bargaining position. Many publishers offer a writer an advance against royalties. The amount depends on the subject matter, the publisher's evaluation of the book's sales potential and your writing background. For a business book by a beginning writer like yourself, an advance of $500 is a realistic amount. The publisher may pay another $500 upon acceptance of the completed manuscript. Your book on business may receive a royalty payment offer of 10 percent on the first 3,000 copies sold and 12 percent after that. The $1,000 you already received would be subtracted from your future royalty payments.

If you will heed a word of caution in your research, be careful about taking large sections from another publication and using them word for word in your own book. You may run into problems with copyright laws. The best way to avoid them is to rewrite information in your own words. Ideas and facts are not copyrightable.

PREPARATION FOR MAILING

An editor may judge your book by the way your manuscript looks. If the margins are uneven, the middle of the *a*s and *e*s are filled in with ink, the pages differ in length and the overall appearance is sloppy, an editor may equate that with the quality of your writing without even reading it. If you don't want to be marked as an amateur, prepare your manuscript like a professional.

If your offering is a full-length book, you should have a title page with your name and address on the upper left-hand corner, the number of words on the upper right-hand corner and the title in full capital letters in the middle of the page followed by your name. The next page should be a table of contents. On the following page, start your book with the name of the first chapter in full caps preceded by Roman numeral I at least a third of the way down the page. Don't number the first pages of each chapter. Other pages should be numbered in the upper right-hand corner.

Indent paragraphs five spaces, double-space your copy and type on one side of the paper only. Margins — left, right, top, and bottom of the page — should be at least one inch. Avoid paper or typewriter ribbon which is off-color. Your paper should be 8½ by 11 inches only. Don't use onion-skin paper.

If you have an arrangement with your publisher where you mail in your chapters as you complete them, you obviously would not be able to compile a table of contents until you have finished the last chapter.

Your magazine article can.be mailed in a 9 by 12-inch Manilla envelope. A book manuscript can be mailed in the box the typing paper came in. Send the pages loose; don't staple or bind them in any way.

Your magazine article does not need a title page. Type your name and address in the upper left-hand corner of the first page of your manuscript. The upper right-hand corner gives the number of words in the story. Then go down a few lines and write the title in full caps followed by your name as you wish it to appear on the article. The story should begin about half-way down the first page a few spaces below your name.

Whenever you submit a full manuscript or article on speculation, you should include return postage. Check with your post office for the special manuscript rate.

Always make at least one copy of your manuscript. The post office has an excellent track record concerning the possibility of losing things in the mail. However, with the amount of work involved, you can't be too careful. You might even want to insure your manuscript.

PHOTOGRAPHY

Photographs can help you sell an article about your company or its product or service. If you have already set up a darkroom and purchased photography equipment for your public relations operation, you are that much ahead of the game.

The top magazines require photographs of a professional quality. However, secondary consumer or trade publications are not so particular about quality.

If you don't want to take your own pictures, there are several alternatives. A good local free-lance photographer may be willing to work with you on speculation. If the article sells, he would be paid for the pictures. You can advise the editor about a good local photographer. If he is interested in the article, he may assign the photographer to illustrate it. You can hire your own commercial photographer to take the pictures, or you may be able to collect some photos that already have been taken of the subject of your story.

If you take your own pictures, get some action into them. Try to get a picture of someone using your product or service. Generally, you don't need permission from the person in the photo or a model release unless the picture is going to be used for advertising purposes.

If possible, try to give your editor more than one picture. Give a choice of vertical or horizontal pictures of every situation to help in page layout.

When you write your captions, be sure to give the full names and titles of everyone in the picture and explain what they are doing. A picture and caption should reinforce, illustrate and amplify the text of your article rather than repeat it.

Protect your photos with cardboard when you place them in an envelope for mailing. Dog-eared photographs aren't much good to an editor. Avoid paper clips or staples that might damage the print.

If you process your own photos, make sure you leave a white border around the picture so the editor can indicate where it should be cropped. Print the entire negative and let the editor decide which part of it to use. She is the one doing the layout for the magazine and knows her own needs as far as space and format are concerned.

When you send a group of portraits for use in the same release, make sure the head sizes are the same. Don't send a cheesecake photo to a publication unless you know that they use such material. If you aren't sure, send a straight photo.

Indicate the source of the photo on the back of the picture, even if it is accompanied by a caption. However, don't write product data on the back of the photo. That type of information should go in the story or caption.

Do not request that your photos be returned. It puts an added burden on the editor and publication. Let them keep the picture. Many publications like to build a photo file and the possibility exists that the photo might be used again. It would give you a double dose of public relations with one photo.

Go easy on the advertising when you are composing the photo. The picture is for a magazine story and not an advertisement. Don't plaster your brand name all over the photo and try to fill the picture with items displaying the name of your company. You shouldn't use the same photo for your magazine story that you use for advertisements.

Your photo sizes should be 8 by 10 inches or 5 by 7 inches. Be wary about using anything smaller than that.

PROVIDING PHOTOS TO THE MEDIA

A related form of public relations is providing photographs to journalists as illustrations for their own magazines and newspaper articles. However, you should be certain that such exposure provides good publicity for your firm. Many of the larger companies have found it worthwhile to maintain their own photo laboratories to help with public relations and promotional activities.

Although your firm may not be large enough to maintain its own photo lab, there is no reason why you couldn't start your own photo file. You could have portraits of all management personnel and pictures of production activities and the plant to hand to the media at their request.

GETTING TO WORK

Now it's your turn. You have most of the basic information you need to write for success, but you are the only one who can make it work. There will be days when you feel like writing the history of the world. Other days, you just won't feel like writing at all. On those latter days, you'll have to pick yourself up by the scruff of the neck and set yourself in front of the typewriter. Even if you produce nothing but garbage, you've still got to write on those days. Like any other activity, the more you write the better you will get.

Prepare a definite working schedule. Some writers do their best work in the wee hours of the morning when the house is quiet and their minds are fresh. Or you might be a night person who comes to life only after dark. Do your own thing as long as you write something every day.

Some people work better if they are writing against a deadline. If the editor of your book or magazine has not given you a deadline, set your own and strive to meet it.

CHAPTER

10

10

Special Problems in Public Relations

Crisis!

You have just picked up the morning paper. There, staring at you from page 1, is the headline:

Baby Dies from Poisoned Nighty!

You make baby wear. Your heart in your mouth, you read on. That poisoned nighty was one of yours.

What do you do now? The poison, traced to the dye used in the cloth, produces a deep rash and respiratory problems. One infant already has died and another is in critical condition. Your product has been pinpointed as the cause.

The suppliers of the dye have admitted their guilt, but you still have a massive public relations problem. Baby clothes from your factory have been shipped to retail stores throughout the East.

How do you deal with such an emergency? First of all, you should already have an emergency public rela-

197

tions plan with a blueprint for swinging into action immediately.

Your first step, to warn the public, is obvious. Don't spare the horses. Spend whatever is necessary to spread the word throughout the country. Enlist the aid of national television, radio and the major newspapers. Designate someone to telephone all the retail outlets so they can remove your product from the shelves.

Then you can concentrate your efforts on repairing the damage.

EMERGENCY PRINCIPLES

The public will judge the quality of your company by the manner in which you react to an emergency. In fact, your firm's efficient and professional response may even create a measure of good will toward your company. The following principles will help you to organize your reaction to an emergency:

1. Draft an emergency public relations plan in advance.
2. Designate *one* trained person to be in charge of emergency operations.
3. Warn the public immediately if a health or safety problem is involved.
4. Work quickly before public opinion solidifies.
5. Spend what is needed to resolve the emergency.
6. Call in outside specialists, if needed.
7. Give the complete story to the media as soon as possible.
8. Don't try to cover up an emergency.
9. Don't speculate to the media.
10. Refute rumors quickly.
11. Notify next-of-kin before identifying victims to media.

When confronted with an emergency, some companies make the mistake of letting everybody help. The president, vice president, director of public relations and other top executives all feel a responsibility to pitch in and lend a hand for the common cause. However, this often results in conflicting statements to the media, crossed wires and various other snafus.

Designate one executive only to be in charge during an emergency. Make that person responsible for all interviews by the print and electronic media, the approval of all news releases and deciding what should be done about situations not covered in the emergency public relations plan.

The person you select to run emergency operations, whether a senior executive officer or the director of public relations, should be given the authority, an adequate and flexible budget and all the equipment and facilities needed to work effectively.

If the situation warrants, you might even bring in an outside individual who is a specialist in the field concerning the nature of the emergency.

It is more important to work quickly than to worry about the cost of damage repair. Public opinion solidifies more and more with every day that passes. A band aid job will make the repair work more costly in the long run.

Probably one of the worst steps that a company can take is to try to cover up a major emergency. Of course, in this day and age, it is well-nigh impossible to keep such a calamity under wraps.

As head of your company, you would do well to follow the example of the airlines or the oil companies in the event of an air disaster or major oil spill. To use the vernacular, spill your guts. Tell the media everything they want to know. This includes the number of casualties, the damage, the cause if you know it, the cost of damage, who is involved, what the company is doing about it and any other details pertinent to the story. Identify the dead as soon as the next-of-kin are notified. People shouldn't learn about the death of a relative through newspaper, radio or television. The media understand this and will cooperate.

If you have not yet determined the cause of the emergency, tell the media that it is under investigation and give them all the details you do have. But don't speculate on the cause.

If you try to cover up or stonewall the media in a major emergency, you will get far more bad publicity than you ever dreamed could exist. They will chip away at the story until all the questions have been answered. Every day you will see another story about the status of their investigation with a rehash of the initial emergency. A former president of the United States paid dearly for an attempt to cover up an investigation.

A policy statement in the Emergency Public and Press Relations Plan of the Tenneco Oil Company makes the following points

> An accident, obviously, can never result in what the company would consider good publicity, and the company is not so naive as to expect any of its spokesmen to turn a bad situation into a good situation. However, generally a bad situation will be made worse by ignoring the news media or trying to hamper their efforts.
>
> Accurate information from a primary source serves our interests better than inaccurate information from a secondary source, the latter often tending to be exaggerated and overstated. When we must take a dose of bad publicity, it is better to release accurate information as quickly and as fully as possible, swallowing our dose all at once instead of having it strung out over a period of days as the press repeatedly uncovers new information and new accusations from uninformed and possibly unfriendly secondary sources.

The statement also emphasizes that the

> public and the news media have a legitimate interest in emergencies. The public has the right to be informed and Tenneco has the duty to see that they get the facts, generally through the news media. If an honest approach of cooperation is extended to the news media, they will treat it objectively, and possibly sympathetically. If they can't get information from us, they will get it from the source they can.

Of course, there are times when it is necessary to withhold information for a while at least. For example,

you might have information about a commercial air-
line crash, but you don't know the flight number. Dis-
closure of such information might create panic among
everyone who has a relative on a flight at that time. Announcements of extortion attempts, ransom demands
and bomb threats also might have to be delayed. But,
even then, explain the legal, security or safety reasons
that make you withhold information. Use the response
of "no comment" as a last resort. That is why your company should have an individual to make decisions in
those uncharted areas of emergency. There is no way to
establish an emergency public relations plan to cover
every situation.

Above all, do not speculate about the causes, dollar
value of losses or any other information related to an
emergency. If you don't know, say so.

THE EMERGENCY PR PLAN

Before you prepare your emergency plan, you
should compile a list of things that could go wrong and
form your plan around them. If you deal with many
combustible materials such as fireworks, fire or explo-
sion may be the greatest hazards at your plant. A manufacturer of insecticides is sitting on a potential time
bomb. Any company that makes or uses chemicals in
its processes is prone to accidents with these substances, as Union Carbide now knows very well.

At one time, I lived near a plant engaged in the
processing of magnesium, an element that burns rapidly and is used in the manufacture of signal flares
and fireworks. Periodically, there would be an explo-
sion at the plant, with ensuing deaths and injuries.
Work was done in a series of small buildings which
collapsed easily when their contents exploded. Need-
less to say, if they had an emergency public relations
plan, their area of vulnerability was much in evidence.

If your area of vulnerability is not quite as obvious
as that of the magnesium plant, you may need outside
assistance to study where your company is prone to

crisis or disaster.

Alan Bernstein (1981) notes that the emergency PR plan is intended to provide the methods, tools and training that ensure:

1. Speedy relief and recovery
2. Reduce uncertainty
3. Minimum liabilities
4. Protection of the organization's image/credibility, thereby its operating relationships; and its ability to start up again after the crisis or disaster

Bernstein also lists psychological objectives:

1. To maintain or improve morale
2. To improve efficiency
3. To create allies from neutrals, neutralize enemies and strengthen and unify existing allies
4. To inform and educate
5. To redirect public interests into more positive areas
6. To build credibility an/or image
7. To establish a sympathetic audience
8. To reduce uncertainty

Your emergency public relations plan might contain an overall policy statement and might specify procedures in special emergency situations. It should cover types of incidents and locations; duties of various personnel including the senior officer, security liaison, PR expert, information center coordinator and other key personnel who must be notified in priority order; equipment and special services for the news media and special audiences such as employees, stockholders, suppliers, customers, mutual aid associations and adjacent industries. It should also plan for approaching families of victims, and the information needs of public relations liaisons. The plan should include referral guides.

The policy statement specifies that someone in your organization has the duty, authority and responsibility to speak on behalf of the organization in case of an emergency.

THE RUMOR MACHINE

There is nothing more damaging than a rampant rumor, an unsupported statement passed from person to person, usually by word-of-mouth. A rumor always gives the impression of truth because it exists wherever a subject is of intense, but temporary interest to an audience and real facts are absent. For example, in the case of the toxic dye in baby clothes, suppose a rumor began to circulate that other types of wearing apparel also were impregnated with the poison? It would cause a general panic.

Rumors must be refuted quickly because they result in scapegoating and blame-placing. They destroy morale, spread disunity, create confusion and stimulate crisis and emergency responses. In fact, persons who spread rumors during a crisis may be enemies of your company who seek to discredit and destroy your firm and its capacity to recover from the emergency.

Find out as much as you can about the rumor and assign the job of refuting it to a specific spokesperson or group with authority and confidence. Use logic and facts and try to reduce the circulation of the rumor. Allow recognized authorities outside the company to help. And make sure the refutation discredits rather than validates the rumor.

THE SATAN RUMOR

Procter & Gamble Company was forced to wrestle with a massive public relations crisis when a vicious rumor charged that the owner of the corporation had made a pact with Satan. If Satan would help him prosper, he would give his heart and soul to Satan when he died, so the rumor went. The company trademark, a moon-and-stars design, also was rumored to be the symbol of Satan. Stuart M. Konkler, Supervisor for

Public Affairs at Procter & Gamble, developed a series of releases as the unfounded rumor spread across the country. He also enlisted the aid of religious leaders to dispel the rumors.

An excerpt from one of his releases follows:

> The stories, which have been around for more than two years, typically report that a P&G executive discussed satanism on a nationally televised talk show. Producers of each of the programs mentioned in the stories have confirmed that no one from P&G has appeared on their program. In recent months, the problem has escalated and P&G now is receiving more than 12,000 calls each month about the rumor. P&G said it has not been able to track down how the rumor got started, but it has received reports of the story from all fifty states. The company said it is taking the problem seriously and is prepared to take legal action if necessary to stop the spread of the stories.
>
> Most people are satisfied that the rumor is false after they get more information, and especially if that information comes from someone they know and trust, the company said. P&G hopes that people will believe the facts coming from religious leaders . . .

One of the leaders was the Rev. Jerry Falwell, host of the national TV and radio program, "Old Time Gospel Hour." Falwell said,

> It is unfortunate that such false accusations are made in the first place, but even more concerning that they can be spread as rumor by people who call themselves Christian. I have discussed these rumors with the Chairman of the Board of Procter & Gamble, who happens to be from my home town in Virginia, and I am certain neither he nor his company is associated in any way with satanism or devil worship. Christians have a responsibility to know the truth before spreading the stories and, in this case, the truth is there is no story to tell. I urge Christians everywhere to help put an end to these unfortunate rumors.

A subsequent release noted that Procter & Gamble had taken legal action against a number of individuals

accused of making statements or distributing literature which claimed that Procter & Gamble supported
Satan and that its trademark was a satanic symbol. The
release also explained how the moon-and-stars design
evolved as a trademark.

Eventually, Konkler and his staff produced a booklet which explained the evolution of the moon-and-
stars as the company trademark. It was distributed to
the media and other interested parties.

The Public Affairs Department at Procter & Gamble
did an outstanding job in its battle against the Satan
rumor. Curiously, the firm came out of the crisis smell-
ing of roses. The company received hundreds of thousands of dollars worth of favorable exposure in both
regional and national trade and consumer media.

I have mentioned certain basic principles that
should be followed in handling a PR crisis. However,
how can a company prepare for a problem such as the
Satan rumor? Like Konkler and his staff, you have to
cope with each aspect of the problem as it unfolds, and
utilize the media to get the true story to the public. It
also strengthens the credibility of your story to obtain
the aid of a person not associated with the company, as
Procter & Gamble did with Falwell and other religious
leaders.

The Satan case has not been the only major public
relations problem for Procter & Gamble. The toxic
shock syndrome scare forced Rely tampons off the market and resulted in a series of lawsuits. Then there was
the problem of Ivory Snow model Marilyn Chambers
appearing in the pornographic movie, "Behind the
Green Door."

IMPLEMENTING THE PR PLAN

Proper communications is one of the most important aspects of an emergency. When a crisis occurs,
there often are two realities: what has happened and
what people think has happened. Quite often a company is not prepared for the latter factor. Therefore, it is

crucial that you quickly meet emergency information demands shaped by the audiences to be addressed, the news media and your own PR planning.

You should maintain control over the physical site of the emergency, including access to the site, the victims, rescue workers and information. Combine security and your news management skills to maintain press discipline to limit the ill-effects of news reporting on the positive steps you have taken in the emergency.

The news media usually hear about an emergency by monitoring official communications or speaking to people. If it is a major event, you can be sure they will be at the site with all staff resources and technical equipment.

DIRECT CONTACT

When the media cover an emergency, they are indirectly reaching the audiences with which you are concerned. However, sometimes your purposes would be better served if you contacted these audiences directly. They include employees, stockholders, government officials, suppliers, customers, adjacent industries, local community groups, families of victims and the victims themselves as they recover or are recovered.

NOTIFYING NEXT-OF-KIN

Always notify the next-of-kin before disclosing to the media the names of those killed or injured. It softens the blow of finding out a loved one has died or been hurt. If possible, deliver the news in person or have a representative of your company approach the family. Make the call between 6 a.m. and 10 p.m., be neat in appearance, be as inconspicuous as possible, be natural in speech and manner, give a brief factual statement about what happened, be alert to adverse reactions and ask if there is anything you can do. The manner in which you perform this delicate public relations task directly reflects the quality of your company.

INFORMATION CENTER

If the emergency is of a major nature, you may want to set up an information center. It should be accessible to the media, but separated from the emergency site, command center, victims, families and rescue workers. The center should contain office, safety, transportation and communications equipment. Plans should be made for newspaper delivery, television sets and radios in the center. You might also consider additional telephone lines or a toll-free line. Besides serving as a base of operations for the media, the information center could be used for briefings, news conferences and interviews by company officials.

POSITIVE NEWS MANAGEMENT

The media don't like the term "news management." However, our goal is to minimize the negative impact that the media may have on the positive outcome of the emergency. So, for want of a better phrase, we will use "news management" to describe your attempts to play down strife and emphasize cooperation. Dealing with the problem will test your skill in the public relations field. You must understand the reporters' jobs and appeal to their sense of civic pride and professionalism. Give them what they need as long as it doesn't interfere with the handling of the emergency.

Sometimes you can facilitate the news management chore by limiting the number of journalists, photographers and broadcasters you allow to enter the emergency site. This practice, knows as press pooling, should be considered only in a major emergency when the number of media representatives on the site is interfering with recovery operations.

With a press pool, you could permit no more than a dozen journalists to cover the emergency on site if they agree to share photographs, footage and information with their colleagues. When forming the press pool, let the journalists select from among their colleagues who will be in the pool. Strive to attain a proper balance of newspaper, radio, and television reporters and photographers.

When you return from the emergency site, give the journalists, photographers and cameramen an opportunity to ask individual questions and grant interviews. Include those who were not in the press pool. This will help all of them to file their own individual stories and they will appreciate this courtesy.

DISSEMINATING INFORMATION

The method and tool you use to disseminate information depends on the nature of the audience you wish to reach. That, in turn, depends on the nature of the emergency. News conferences, briefings and open meetings will spread the word to the general circulation media. If more speed in reaching the public is warranted, broadcasts, including the Emergency Broadcasting System, regularly scheduled broadcasts and public service announcements, may be the answer. Public speaking will give you access to a specific audience and outreach will get you to an elusive audience. Employee briefings and personal visits should be used for specific purposes.

News releases, telephones, messengers, telephone answering devices, teletype systems, amateur radio, leaflets, posters, advertisements, word-of-mouth, readiness films and alarms and alert signals are the tools at your disposal. Some, like the news release and advertisement, will disseminate information to a general audience. Others such as the telephone and amateur radio are designed for specific or selected audiences. The latter instrument was the only means of reaching the outside world after the 1985 earthquake devastated Mexican cities.

BE PREPARED

The Boy Scout motto, "Be Prepared," may sound trite to some, but there is a lot of truth in it. The

emergency public relations plan is one way to be prepared for a possible disaster at your plant. Readiness
films on preparing for crisis or disaster is another.
They may be obtained from both public and private
sources including insurance companies, major corporations, Civil Defense, Red Cross and the Federal Emergency Management Administration.

CASE HISTORIES

The Tylenol crisis, like Procter & Gamble's handling of the Satan rumor, is an example of good public
relations and advance preparation. Seven people died
in Chicago after taking poisoned Tylenol. Although
Johnson & Johnson was not at fault, the company had a
very difficult PR problem. The firm immediately re-
moved all Tylenol from the market even though the
product was and is extremely important to the company. Johnson & Johnson had formed in advance a strategy that the protection of the reputation of the company
and the product was of prime importance. It takes years
to build a reputation and customer confidence and a
break in that trust would take years to rebuild. The
trust is based on the presumption that the company is
concerned about its customers and will not place their
health in jeopardy. The company may have lost some
sales, but the manner in which it handled the problem
maintained public confidence in its reputation. Johnson & Johnson then reintroduced the Tylenol brand and
recovered a substantial portion of its previous market.

The Girl Scout cookie crisis is a classic example of
poor public relations and no advance planning. In 1984,
the organization received numerous reports of product
tampering such as pins in cookies. Executive directors
of local Girl Scout Councils began speaking to the media, giving the impression of product contamination or
a conspiracy to sabotage sales. However, all the incidents were local and had no particular pattern. As a result, the publicity unjustly damaged cookie sales that
year. If the Girl Scout organization had trained in ad-

vance one spokesperson to handle such a crisis, the damage could have been reduced substantially. An organization's reputation hinges on how well it responds to a crisis with a trained spokesperson who can take care of the situation calmly and professionally.

The Three-Mile Island case is another example of an organization failing to get its act together. For days after the threatened meltdown of the nuclear power plant, all the involved government agencies were issuing their own statements and comments. The front pages of newspapers were dominated with contradictory and inaccurate information because they didn't centralize the spokesperson function. Although there never was real danger to the community, the multiple spokesperson situation virtually created so much public panic that the term "environmental impact" acquired a whole new dimension. The White House finally stepped in and centralized the public spokesperson function, but the damage had been done.

DOW'S RAILWAY CRISES

Dow is another firm which performed well in two crisis situations, both involving derailments and chemicals. However, the one which posed little or no danger to the public created the greatest problems. A comparison of the two incidents illustrates the need for fast, accurate and properly explained news information.

In November 1979, 27 of 106 Dow cars were derailed at Mississauga, Ontario. They contained propane, toluene, styrene monomer, caustic soda and chlorine. The accident occurred in a dense population area adjacent to the largest news media center in Canada. The hazardous chemicals were a serious public health threat. Many well-organized emergency workers arrived at the scene, security at the derailment site was established quickly, chemical experts appeared in a few hours and scores of news media representatives converged on the area. An information center was set up and media briefings were conducted several times a day by highly credible senior government officials supported by technical experts. Evacuations were orderly and there was no evidence of public panic. The situation was well under control. Soon the site was cleaned up without mishap.

Another derailment at MacGregor, Manitoba, in March 1980 contrasted sharply with the Mississauga incident. The accident occurred at 1:30 a.m. in a lightly populated rural area. There was a heavy snowfall, high winds and bitter cold. The nearest major media center was 100 kilometers away or at least an hour and a half by car in good weather. Among the derailed cars were twelve containing vinyl chloride monomer (VCM) from Dow's Fort Saskatchewan plant. There were no fires, explosions, injuries or deaths.

Because of the low temperature and the short term of exposure, the VCM represented little risk to human health. The weather prevented Dow's emergency response technical experts from getting to the site until ten hours after the derailment. Senior railway officials arrived at the site before them. Manitoba environmental officials also were involved. Two VCM leaks were discovered, one shortly after the derailment and the other four days later.

The accident attracted a lot of news coverage during the first week. Reporters' questions were answered and technical meetings were held. There were no formal press briefings because there was no significant public health or environmental hazard involved that was not under control.

The problem occurred when a university professor who happened to be in the area at the time issued a public statement. She contended there would have been a mass evacuation of a 10-mile radius if a derailment involving a leaking VCM car had happened in the United States because the chemical has been proven to cause cancer! The media had a field day with the information. The politicians, environmental and labor groups joined the wave of indignation, alleging a cover up.

Apparently, no one checked the accuracy of the professor's statement. The facts were that repeated exposure of plant workers to high concentrations of VCM gas over a working lifetime — a chronic exposure condition — was discovered in 1974 to cause a rare form of liver cancer. These exposures probably were thousands of times greater and for much longer durations than those at the Manitoba derailment site.

After several meetings with technical experts, environmentalists, railway experts, Dow officials, a pharmacologist, scientists, politicians, media and the general public, and a full-page, full-disclosure newspaper ad on "The Facts about Vinyl Chloride Monomer," the controversy was resolved. At the final meeting, a resident proposed a commendation to all those who worked on the derailment clean-up. He was loudly applauded.

However, the experience taught Dow several lessons. In such a situation involving chemicals, hazardous or not, the media must be fully informed frequently and accurately from the outset until the spill is cleaned up. If those prerequisites are not met, a public information vacuum will develop and pseudo-experts will move in to fill that gap with speculation and inflammatory statements. Silence implies guilt, justified or not. It is not enough just to provide the scientific truth of a situation. Details also must be given. Reporters must face deadlines hour by hour with developing stories, and many stories have to be reported piecemeal.

Dow is ready for the next crisis. They have a mobile chemicals newsroom in two suitcases ready to run at a moment's notice to set up a modest news media information center. The suitcases travel with the emergency response crews to the site.

THE SHUTDOWN

There is nothing worse than a plant shutdown, especially in a company town that has depended both economically and socially on one company. The problem has posed a PR challenge for decades. The goal, of course, is to minimize the negative impact on everyone involved and to maintain good will.

Public relations practitioners recommend that a company develop advance phase-out plans in the same way as it prepares crisis or emergency plans. You should develop the plan jointly with local government officials, business leaders and social service agencies with the understanding that you are developing the plan as a contingency in case of an unexpected financial downturn or company reorganization. The plan should consider the needs for community development and financial diversification.

In a shutdown crisis, you would do well to address certain principles in order to leave a good taste in the mouths of the people you leave behind. You should understand the psychology of the community and the workforce. Try to develop a unified business structure in the community. Become personally involved in the community network. Attend meetings and contact as many persons as possible.

As you establish programs, create resident responsibility for them. Program heads should live in the community. And use local persons as much as possible. That is one method of coping with hostility, which will run deep. Develop the program as a separate entity from the company. If you can't develop a long-term program in depth, forget about it.

PRICE RESISTANCE

When customers at your retail store say, "I love it, but it costs too much," you've got to equip your sales staff to come back with the proper answer. Among other things, you can train your personnel to emphasize quality and service. The quality in your merchandise should be apparent. As far as the service is concerned, it should be demonstrated.

If you continue to draw criticism about your prices

for quality merchandise, you might consider the possibility of relocating your store in an exclusive neighborhood, or you might have better luck selling your product and capturing the up-scale market by placing ads in the *New Yorker*. Train your sales staff to answer objections to price, quality, service, delivery schedules or other aspects of your retail business.

You might even *raise* your prices. Think of the news stories that would provoke*!*.

CHAPTER

11

11

Sampling Public Opinion

How do you measure public relations? You can't weigh it. You can't take a yardstick and mark off a certain number of inches of PR. You can't put it in a graduated bucket, although some people may insist you can.

Of course, you can always measure bad public relations by the amount of antagonism toward your company, but that kind of PR doesn't help us very much. It's the good public relations that concerns us. There are ways to measure good public relations. You may not get an exact measurement because public relations is an inexact science.

The public relations practitioner works with attitudes, striving to favorably impact attitudes of a variety of publics. Compared with other marketing communications techniques such as direct mail and advertising, there still is a certain amount of guesswork.

However, methods of measuring public relations

results are becoming more and more sophisticated as company executives with lean budgets examine every component of the marketing mix to assure that they are receiving value for money. Public relations programs, at one time taken for granted on the basis of cost-efficiency, now must prove their worth. A great amount of publicity no longer is enough to satisfy them.

QUANTITATIVE MEASUREMENT

Despite advances in the techniques of calculating public relations, the quantity of exposure still is an important factor. For example, a national public relations program for a well-established product with a brand name may be concerned only with obtaining as many brand-name mentions as possible in media reaching the product's primary target audiences. The idea is that these mentions will make people more aware of the product and the advertising will be more effective.

The quantitative techniques include measurement of:

1. The column inches and air time generated by public relations efforts
2. Number of stories placed in publications or broadcast on the air
3. The known circulation and viewership of the placements
4. Multiplying circulation/viewership figures by a certain factor to determine the maximum number of people reached by a specific placement. The figure is computed on the basis of a rule-of-thumb estimate of two and one-half persons reading each paper or magazine
5. The number of target markets reached by publicity
6. Media statistics defining how many primary consumers were exposed to the publicity and how much of it was wasted
7. How much the space or air time would cost if it was purchased as advertising

QUALITATIVE MEASUREMENT

If the objective of a marketing public relations program is to boost sales, qualitative measurement techniques could be used. They include:

1.   Testing before and after evaluates marketing effectiveness. It is seldom used just for public relations purposes because of the cost. However, it is possible to piggy-back on market tests to get some idea of the effectiveness of your PR program. The pretesting identifies overall awareness and attitude and perceived strengths and weaknesses. The post-testing is difficult to interpret because it is hard to pinpoint the reasons for possible increases in awareness, acceptance and trial. There could be varying degrees of public relations, or advertising. Sometimes the results can be clarified with quantitative data.

2.   Comparing controlled markets involves sales results in test markets. One test where PR was part of the marketing mix is compared with another where it was not included. Roy R. Bumsted (1983) cites the example of a program to educate the public and trade about the merits of a new reusable paper towel. A spokesperson, a well-known home economist, was hired for interviews by radio, TV and newspapers in five selected markets. The sales results were then compared with five markets where the towel was introduced without the PR program. In the markets with PR, the penetration increased 14 percent and average sales were 10 percent higher. Yet, PR costs showed only a 7 percent increase in the marketing budget.

3.   Direct response from customers to a PR effort can be a cost-effective means of evaluating publicity. Bumsted outlines the case of Evelyn Wood Reading Dynamics placing one of its top students on the "Tonight Show" to demonstrate her incredible reading ability. Following the show, more than 15,000 people called Evelyn Wood offices for course information. All cited the "Tonight Show" demonstration.

4.   Communications with sales representatives is

a less scientific, but an effective way of evaluating public relations. The sales force, by virtue of its field operations, is in an ideal position to judge the impact of a publicity campaign.

BENCHMARK SURVEYS

If you begin with adequate research, you can conduct more meaningful and intelligent PR programming. You should know the region in question, the composition of the region, what the publics in the region think of your company, and what effect previous communications from your firm have had on those publics.

One way to collect this information is through a benchmark survey. Such a survey, which provides a reference point to help you measure results of new PR efforts, frequently takes the form of a communications audit. The audit is an evaluation, a perception survey of all key publics to find out what they think of your firm, its communication techniques, the messages, and attitude response to the actions of your company. You can carry out the communications audit by mail, telephone, personal interviews or a combination of any or all of them.

A communications audit can be particularly effective in determining how your company is perceived in comparison with your competition. Repeat the audit a year later to see if progress has been made as a result of adjustments prompted by your initial audit.

You can also use your benchmark survey as a reference point when you measure your space and air time exposure. The degree to which the exposure has improved over previous efforts offers a definite measurement of current public relations effectiveness.

The benchmark survey method will aid your comparison of the cost-effectiveness of PR by the print and electronic media versus advertising. It will demonstrate that you are receiving important value for your promotional publicity dollars.

The publics that you choose to survey in your audit also are important. They should include the stockholders, financial community, financial press, investment bankers and security analysts. Each has a different set of concerns about your company and should be surveyed for their perceptions of its successes, failures, management personnel and style, effectiveness in the marketplace, research and development, long-range planning, marketing and merchandising effectiveness, product or service superiority, and communications effectiveness.

If you have a number of plant locations, you should conduct perception research relative to community relations. Customers' evaluations of your company's products and services and employees' and suppliers' attitudes all should be included in your survey.

And don't forget the media. The peer-group approach is especially important in determining media perceptions of how your company compares with the competition.

An evaluation of your existing communications is also necessary for your survey. You also may want to include the municipal, state and federal governments in your survey to get the official perception of your program.

DEFINING THE IMPACT

In recent years, the emphasis on public relations measurement has been slowly shifting from output to impact. Practitioners are beginning to realize that if public relations is to be accepted by management, play a larger part in the communications mix and command larger budgets at the same time, it is important to increase the focus on impact.

However, they still have a ways to go. In 1981–1982, Research and Forecasts, Inc., conducted a survey among senior communications executives in the Fortune 1,000 companies. It indicated only 38 percent of the respondents measured PR by impact. Practitioners in smaller companies are even less likely to evaluate public relations in this manner.

The traditional method of measuring public relations has involved a body count of clippings, lineage, events or minutes of air time. However, ignoring the impact factor is like making an assumption that a news story is a good one because it sweeps over a full page or because it consumes more air time. Or it could be like pouring millions of dollars into a government program that benefits no one. You have to measure excellence in public relations by its effect, as well as by the effort that went into it.

Jacob Jacoby and Wayne D. Hoyer (1982) make that point. Although the observation was drawn in the context of advertising, it is also appropriate to the output versus impact issue in public relations:

> The investigation again reveals a fundamental truth: The mere provision of information does not automatically mean it will have any effect, much less the intended effect. . . . Rather the receiver/viewer brings a storehouse of past experience and ongoing mental set to each communication transaction and tends to interpret and misinterpret communications in terms of these mental phenomena.

There is no question that there must be output before there is impact. Messages, points of view, ideas, information or brand names cannot have impact until they reach the various publics. They certainly will not be absorbed through osmosis. However, if the communication does not result in some effect on the target audience, it is merely an academic exercise. There is no value in it.

In this day and age, the manager who authorizes a public relations program also wants some results. He or she wants to know what has happened to the audience, not just how many placements in the print media or how much air time in the electronic media were generated. Consequently, the burden on the PR practitioner to show his worth is becoming heavier and heavier.

Despite the apparent need for impact measurement, there has not been a great deal of progress in developing practical methods of achieving it. The profession's fear of having its performance measured may be one reason why these techniques have not gone full speed ahead. That is a normal human reaction. Consider the controversy which raged for years in the teaching profession about merit increases in salary structures and teacher evaluation. Could you imagine the opposition to a system for evaluating the performances of doctors and lawyers? In 1981, members of the Chicago Chapter of the Public Relations Society of America were surveyed on the idea that most practitioners fear measurement. The results were that 54 percent did not disagree with the idea against 46 percent who disagreed with the notion.

Cost is another reason why methods of measuring public relations effectiveness have not developed rapidly. Smaller PR programs require relatively greater expenditures to calculate their impact. However, it is possible to measure selected portions of a public relations program. Feedback on a small scale could help a PR practitioner to evaluate an entire program.

We know that cost-effectiveness comparisons of programs and program elements may be achieved by impact measurement rather than by output measurement. By measuring the impact, we can also determine the reasons behind a program's effectiveness. We can understand what works, what doesn't and why. Thus, in designing our PR program, we can choose the elements with the greatest chance of affecting the largest number of the target audience. If we don't have some indication of the effectiveness of the various elements, much of the design would be pure guesswork.

In addition to determining which elements of the PR program are the most effective, impact measurement also can pinpoint the limits to which public relations can be translated into attitude change or strengthening. For example, research has shown that even when motivated, a work force is not necessarily more productive.

We oversimplify the relationship when we say that employee motivation programs are directly responsible for increases in production.

CASE HISTORIES

Lloyd Kirban (1983) cites an extensive in-house program conducted by Burson-Marsteller to evaluate the feasibility and utility of impact measurement. Three studies were included in the program. Two applied separate-sample before and after testing where random samples of the target audience are surveyed before and after the activity. The other involved after-testing only with the addition of parallel measurements with a control group. The firm dealt with actual programs or elements as they were implemented and the measurements were in natural settings with non-recruited samples.

One of the problems in making an accurate assessment of a PR activity is isolating its effects from those caused by outside factors. To minimize the chances that these factors would contaminate the measurements, the readings were taken by telephone just before the activity and immediately after it. The target audience was defined by relevant characteristics such as car drivers, chief financial decision-makers in households, annual incomes of at least $25,000, executives with production-related titles and exposure to the means of communication, such as readers of a particular publication, viewers of a broadcast or attendees of a show. After experimentation, the firm finally decided on a minimum of 200 persons per sample so the results could be attributed to the activity and not to chance.

In the first case, a pictorial article was placed in the October 1980 *Ladies Home Journal*. The article focused on fall fashions for women in business, concentrating on increasing women's awareness of Celanese Fibers Marketing Company's Arnel and Fortrel fibers. The particular issue of the magazine, which had a circulation of 3.5 million, contained no advertising for those brands. Just before the issue was released, a telephone survey was conducted of women readers of the magazine in four cities. They were asked what fibers they associated with women's clothes. A week after publication, a comparable number of women were asked the same question. There were substantial increases in both the Arnel and Fortrel brand names, showing that the pictorial approach was successful.

The second case measured the impact of the spokesperson's performance and also demonstrated the diagnostic benefits of impact measurement. A media tour was arranged for a mechanic from the Fram Corporation, which makes products for the automotive aftermarket. The firm wanted to project an image with car buyers and maintainers as being consumer-oriented with such interests as saving gas, increasing the lives of cars and lowering driving costs.

Before the mechanic spokesman's appearance on a talk show, a telephone survey located regular viewers of the show who drove a car. They were asked a series of questions related to the message the spokesman was to communicate during the show. Another sample of viewers with the same characteristics as the first was questioned within thirty-six hours after the show. The after-survey showed that significantly more of the viewers had a favorable impression of the company's customer orientation than before the broadcast.

However, one aspect of the telephone survey puzzled Burson-Marsteller. There was no opinion change on some of the questions. Further investigation revealed that the spokesperson had not covered those message points in his talk. With this research, the spokesperson was able to adjust his presentation.

The third case involved the generation of awareness, interest and sales for a completely new application of Knox Gelatin introduced in 1981 by the Thomas J. Lipton Company in Canada. The firm found that Knox Gelatin is a highly nutritious plant food, safe for both plants and people applying it.

The product was introduced through a direct mail and publicity campaign in a control-test market aproach. The company used a variety of media and methods. It did not promote the new application in a number of provinces. A well-known Canadian personality in the home gardening field promoted the product through a media tour in some of the provinces. The firm used only publicity in the print media in others. In still others, the company gave it the full treatment including print, broadcast and media tour with direct mail. Targetting an audience of house-plant gardeners and other gelatin users, the company measured impact through surveys and sales monitoring.

There was no need to test the market before the activity because the application of Knox Gelatin for plant food was unique. After the campaign, the use of gelatin for plant good was reported to be substantial. In the provinces where there was just a media tour, the results were lower than in the provinces where they got the full publicity exposure and direct mail.

The research also indicated the confusion in the minds of the public between publicity and advertising. A substantial proportion of those aware of Knox Gelatin as a plant food attributed their information to magazine advertising and, to a lesser degree, to other print and broadcast advertising. There was no advertising for the product.

Sales also were substantially higher than in previous years in the provinces where there had been a promotional program as compared with the provinces where the product had not been promoted as a plant food. In addition, the sales increases were proportionately higher in the provinces where there had been more promotional publicity.

In evaluating the effectiveness of their programs, Burson-Marsteller came to several conclusions. While impact measurement can be a valuable tool for company management and PR practitioners, there are difficulties because of lack of control over the substance and timing of public relations and isolating its impact from other factors in the same environment. In a given program, all messages do not make an impression on the target audience because some things are of interest to the audience and some are not. Thus, the success of a program cannot be measured in all or nothing terms. The firm also noted that the practitioner should apply basic communications concepts such as audience involvement, information overload, selective perception and strength of commitment to a diagnosis of public relations' performance.

A nationwide publicity campaign competes with many related and unrelated communications hitting the target audience, which may interfere with the impact of your own campaign. Thus, it may be difficult to attribute changes in attitudes or awareness to your own. Burson-Marsteller also pointed out that what is effective in one location may not be effective in another.

Other considerations resulting from the studies included the possible development of a data base of case histories in impact measurement to determine the amount of change one can expect from given PR programs, a better understanding of the duration of the program's impact and whether the same samples of persons can be used in both before and after tests. Evidence suggests the same people can be used when the communications objective does not include increasing awareness. This would have a direct bearing on the cost because, if such were the case, only half the people would be needed.

There is also the question of interaction between public relations and other forms of communication such as advertising, in-store promotions and direct mail. Does PR supplement other types of communications and, if so, to what degree?

Public relations has been accepted because management believes it is a useful and effective communications tool. However, its future may depend on the extent to which its effectiveness can be measured.

THE KETCHUM PUBLICITY TRACKING MODEL

They have a machine for everything these days so why not have one for measuring public relations? Ketchum Public Relations, a New York City-based firm, has developed the Ketchum Publicity Tracking Model, which goes beyond traditional accounting methods such as measuring column inches, broadcast time and total audiences reached. The Ketchum model, a computer model, can tell a client exactly what she will get for the dollars she spends by calculating a publicity exposure index, the amount of target audience exposure received and the degree to which planned messages were delivered to the target audience.

Paul H. Alvarez (1983) explains how the client and firm plan a PR campaign to be evaluated by the model. They agree upon standards of performance in the number of gross impressions to be achieved within the target audience and the key messages to be delivered to that audience. The company's computer is programmed with audience statistics from media in 120 top national markets. Performance standards for a given program and campaign results also are programmed into the computer.

Printed out by media category, the results show the target audience reached based on numerical values assigned to various selling points in the copy of the message delivered to the audience. Two evaluative numbers, the overall exposure index and the overall value index, are produced by the computer. The degree to which the index is above or below standard index for the campaign of 1.00 indicates to what extent performance was above or below the norm. The tracking model demonstrates in advance what a publicity program will do. In other words, it helps in the decision of whether or not a program is worth carrying out or what it needs to be successful.

The Ketchum model is useful to a certain extent. It evaluates past performance with a certain set of selling points and media. However, in order to determine the actual impact of your own program, you would have to use qualitative measurement techniques such as testing before and after or comparing controlled markets.

IN-HOUSE OR OUT?

As head of your company, I bet you've been mumbling to yourself as you read this chapter. "You think I'm going to tie up half of my company on the telephone making market surveys to see if people are reading our news releases. You may not believe this, but we've got a few other little duties like manufacturing a product and managing a company." You're absolutely right. Because the necessary expertise is more specialized, particularly if you want to measure the impact of your public relations efforts, the argument for an external PR agency is stronger. You might follow the same procedure outlined in Chapter 3 to find a suitable agency to measure the qualitative effects of your PR. The same market research agencies and consultants can do the work.

However, you might consider some quantitative measurement. It doesn't take a great deal of effort to clip a few stories from the newspaper, magazine or other publications and monitor TV and radio broadcasts if you think something about your company may be on the air. The print and electronic media would be more than happy to provide data about circulation, broadcast range and the number of persons they reach, and telephone calls to their respective offices would provide information to help you compare costs of advertising with publicity.

If you are the head of a moderate-sized or larger firm, your marketing director might even have some ideas how you could piggy-back on market tests to obtain some data on the impact of your publicity. There is no reason why you can't have a chat with your sales staff. They should have some ideas about what the public thinks of your company and if your publicity is effective.

NUTS AND BOLTS

You know your company's resources. If you really think you'd like to take a crack at impact measurement, let's get on with it. In preparing a survey without professional help, the first step is to decide what you want to find out. Then you should boil it down so the really necessary facts can be obtained with as few questions as possible. One of the greatest problems in do-it-yourself polls is that they try to put too much information in them. Make sure the survey is honest. A common objection to do-it-yourself polls is that the questions are loaded to support preconceived theories.

The survey should be as objective as possible. Begin with a know-nothing attitude because you are conducting the poll to learn, not to prove. Strive for accuracy by including questions to check against known facts.

You should poll enough people in the area in question to get a reliable sample. Even then, the results may not be valid unless those selected for the survey are representative of the various groups which comprise the public. In its case studies, Burson-Marsteller decided on a minimum of 200 persons per sample after experimentation with various sample sizes. The weighing of the sample is highly technical and very important. It is really a job for professionals. This is especially true when the purpose of the poll is to test a cross section of the public before and after a public relations program. Public opinion pollsters contend that the sample should be a miniature edition of the larger public.

The telephone probably is the most reliable and efficient method of conducting your survey because of the immediate response. It is also the most expensive. Other methods are mailed questionnaire surveys and coupon returns. Coupon returns are effective in reaching a selected audience such as those on your newsletter mailing list, suppliers, stockholders, employees, customers and others. Questionnaires also are effective for specific audiences. But, like the coupons, the

rate of response may not be high enough for a meaningful reading. Also, returns may come only from those
with an axe to grind.

CONCLUSION

As far as this book is concerned, you are nearing
the end, but for your company, it is the beginning of a
new era in public relations. You have learned how to
construct a positive image for your company, its product or service. You have also been advised to do your
good work first before calling attention to it. That advice has been coupled with a warning not to rely on
gimmicks.

With the marketing concept, you were introduced
to the principles of consumer and profit orientation
and the coordination and integration of corporate efforts. Identifying the target market and selecting the
appropriate blend of marketing activities were other
guidelines offered to you for a successful program.

You have been given criteria for selecting the right
person to head your public relations program and how
to set up your own PR operation. If the circumstances
warrant, you were shown how to select an external
agency to do your PR, how to monitor that agency and
what it will cost.

You were introduced to the tools of public relations, shown how to select the right one for a specific
job and how to use it. You also were advised how to recognize a good news story and how to get along with
the media.

In the chapter on photography, you received some
tips on how to compose pictures that will be used by
the media, how to hold a camera and how to set up a
darkroom. If you don't wish to take your own pictures,
the various options in obtaining photos of your company personnel and activities were outlined.

The need for good community relations was emphasized. You were shown how to develop a mutually
beneficial relationship between your company and the

community, how to conduct public service projects, the value of membership in service clubs, professional organizations, trade and technical associations, employers' and manufacturers' associations, civic clubs and social clubs. The same chapter touched upon your company's possible contributions to education and religion. Also, you learned how to plan open houses and exhibits, welcome visitors to your plant, deal with customers, and win community acceptance. The value of person-to-person contact was stressed, and you were given some advice on how to run an economic education program in your community.

As an entrepreneur, your compliance with the affirmative action program may be required by law. However, it is also good business and good public relations, you were told. You were given some case histories to back up that contention.

Direct person-to-person contact is one of the best ways of projecting a favorable image of your company. However, it is not always possible to speak personally to every individual who should receive your company's message. The next best thing is talking to large numbers of persons. For that reason, you were given some tips on writing and delivering speeches and setting up a speakers bureau in your company.

Writing magazine articles and books about your company and its activities or hiring a ghostwriter to do it are excellent forms of public relations. You were offered some guidelines on how to select a story idea and find a publisher.

You learned how to deal with a crisis or cope with special problems that threaten your company and its product. The chapter also reported case histories to illustrate how other companies faced these difficulties. Finally, you were shown that it is possible to measure the impact of public relations as well as the output.

There you are, Mr. Company President. You have the tools and the knowledge to conduct a successful public relations campaign for your company. Got to it. You're on your own.

BIBLIOGRAPHY

Bibliography

Adams, Alexander B. *Handbook of Practical Public Relations.* Thomas Y. Crowell Co., New York. 1965.

Advance. National Headquarters. The American Legion. Indianapolis, Ind. Vol. 27 No. 7. July, 1984.

Alvarez, Paul H. "And Now Comes Chapter III." *Public Relations Journal.* July, 1983.

America, Richard F. "Public Relations and Affirmative Action." *Public Relations Quarterly.* Summer, 1983.

Aspley, John C. *The Dartnell Public Relations Handbook.* The Dartnell Press. Chicago, Ill. 1961.

Beginnings of Photographic Composition. Eastman Kodak Co. 1979.

Bernstein, Alan B. *The Emergency Public Relations Manual.* PASE, Inc. New Brunswick, N.J. 1981.

Bumsted, Roy R. "How to Improve Public Relations Measurement." *Tips & Tactics*, a supplement of *PR Reporter*. PR Publishing Co., Inc. Dudley House. Exeter, N.H. Vol. 21. No. 4. Feb. 21, 1983.

Burger, Chester. *Effective Public Relations*. Cutlip, Center and Broom. 1985.

Cato, Forrest W. "Procter & Gamble and the Devil." *Public Relations Quarterly*. Fall, 1982.

Cohen, William A. and Reddick, Marshall E. *Successful Marketing for Small Business*. AMACOM, New York City. 1981.

Deeb, Marie F. Affirmative action report to Thomas College, Waterville, Maine. September, 1984.

Easton, Thomas A. *How to Write a Readable Business Report*. Dow Jones-Irwin. Homewood, Ill. 1983.

Ferguson, David. Lecture to Maine Public Relations Council. Portland, Maine. June 27, 1985.

Fisher, Anne B. "Businessmen Like to Hire by the Numbers." *Fortune*. September, 1985.

Fucini, Joseph J. & Fucini, Suzy. *Entrepreneurs*. G. K. Hall & Co. Boston. 1985.

Gill, Gerald R. *Meanness Mania: The Changed Mood*. Howard University Press, Washington, D.C. 1980.

Gorney, Carole. "Steel Shutdown in Lackawanna: A Case Study." *Public Relations Quarterly*. Summer, 1985.

Jacoby, Jacob and Hoyer, Wayne D. "Viewer Miscomprehension of Televised Communication: Selected Findings." *Journal of Marketing*. Vol. 46. No. 4. Fall, 1982.

Kirban, Lloyd. "Showing What We Do Makes a Difference." *Public Relations Quarterly*. Fall, 1983.

Kroger, William. "Disabled Workers Are No Handicap to Business." *Nation's Business*. May, 1979.

Lapin, Lawrence. *Statistics for Modern Business Decisions*. Harcourt, Brace Jovanovich, Inc. New York. 1978.

Mahoney, Tom and Hession, Rita. *Public Relations for Retailers*. The Macmillan Co. New York. 1949.

McCarthy, E. Jerome. *Basic Marketing: A Managerial Approach*. Richard D. Irwin, Inc. Homewood, Ill. 1975.

NCAA Public Relations Manual. National Collegiate Athletic Association. Shawnee Mission, Kan. 1981.

O'Dwyer, Jack. *Jack O'Dwyer's Newsletter*.

O'Dwyer, Jack. *O'Dwyer's Directory of Public Relations Firms*.

Palmquist, Ron. Personal interview. Cape Elizabeth, Maine. July 2, 1985.

Pines, Wayne L. "How to Handle a PR Crisis. Five Dos and Five Don'ts." *Public Relations Quarterly*. Summer, 1985.

Rotman, Morris B. *Opportunities in Public Relations*. VGM Career Horizons, a Division of National Textbook Co. Lincolnwood, Ill. 1983.

Rudelius, William; Erickson, W. Bruce and Bakula, William J., Jr. *An Introduction to Contemporary Business*. Harcourt Brace Jovanovich, Inc. New York. 1976.

Soderberg, Norman R. *Public Relations Practices of Maine Mutual Savings Banks*, A Thesis in Business Management. 1980.

Stephenson, D.R. "How to Turn Pitfalls Into Opportunities in Crisis Situations." *Public Relations Quarterly*. Fall, 1982.

Strenski, James B. "Measuring Public Relations Results." *Public Relations Quarterly*. Summer, 1980.

Thomas, Clarence. "Current Litigation Trends and Goals of the EEOC. *"Labor Law Journal*. April, 1983.

Warner, Jr., Rawleigh & Silk, Leonard S. *The 1978 Benjamin F. Fairless Memorial Lectures, Ideals in Collision, The Relationship Between Business & the News Media*. Carnegie-Mellon New York-Guilford, Surrey. 1979.

The Writer. The Writer, Inc. Boston. February, 1985.

Writer's Market. Edited by Jane Koester & Rose Adkins. Writer's Digest. Cincinnati, Ohio. 1974.

INDEX

Index

DATE DUE

JUL 17 2007			